THERAPY IN MUSIC
FOR
HANDICAPPED CHILDREN

Paul Nordoff was an American pianist and composer who at one time combined university teaching with composition for concert hall and theatre. He was so impressed by the scope of music therapy, however, that he decided it was the only worthwhile work for a twentieth-century musician and gave up this career to devote his life to it. He died in the mid-1970s.

Clive Robbins was working in special education at Sunfield Children's Home when he met Dr Nordoff. They went on to work together as a team for many years, first at Sunfield, later at Pennsylvania University and with backward children in Philadelphia. Clive Robbins and his wife, Carol, also a music therapist, continue the work and are directing the Nordoff Music Therapy Clinic at New York University.

BY THE SAME AUTHORS:

MUSIC THERAPY IN SPECIAL EDUCATION
(an instructional manual on group activities)

John Day Company Inc. Publishers, New York City

THERAPY IN MUSIC FOR HANDICAPPED CHILDREN

Paul Nordoff
and
Clive Robbins

With a Foreword by
BENJAMIN BRITTEN

LONDON
VICTOR GOLLANCZ LTD
1992

First published in Great Britain October 1971
by Victor Gollancz Ltd,
14 Henrietta Street, London WC2E 8QJ

First published in Gollancz Paperbacks May 1985
Second impression September 1985
Third impression March 1992

ISBN 0-575-03658-3

Some of the content of this book derives from an earlier
book: *Music Therapy for Handicapped Children: Investigations and Experiences*, Rudolf Steiner Publications,
New York, 1965. For the present book the former text has
been completely rewritten, expanded, and reorganized by
the inclusion of much supplementary material which has
become available since that time.

Printed in Great Britain by
St Edmundsbury Press Ltd, Bury St Edmunds, Suffolk

To Mary Curtis Zimbalist, and her son,
Curtis Bok, who believed in this work
from the very beginning.

NOTE

The musical material referred to in the text is as follows:

Pif-Paf-Poltrie
Children's Play-Songs, Volumes One and Two
The Three Bears
The Story of Artaban
Fun For Four Drums
The Children's Christmas Play
Spirituals for Children to Sing and Play
Play-Songs with Resonator Bells
The Twenty-third Psalm
The Musicians of Bremen

These works by Paul Nordoff and Clive Robbins are published by Theodore Presser Company, Bryn Mawr, Pa., U.S.A. They are available in Europe from Alfred A. Kalmus Ltd., 2/3 Fareham St., London, W.1.

This book was originally published when the term "mongoloid" was widely used and before the diagnosis of Down's syndrome was universally adopted.

CONTENTS

FOREWORD

This is an intensely moving, as well as a very important book. It is the story of a distinguished American composer virtually stopping his "abstract" composing, as it were, in mid-career and using his talents and energies to discover ways of helping by music mentally deprived children. I imagine Paul Nordoff previously knew little of this tragic side of life, and it was a shattering experience for him to come into contact with it: a glance at the illustrations at the back of this book can give a hint of that. This quietly written account of his and Mr. Robbins' patient experiments, their journeys into the obscured world of these children, will not easily be forgotten.

I am not qualified to comment on the importance of the psychological cures that these two men have achieved, nor of the extension of diagnosis. But this I can say—the book is as well highly important for musicians, particularly composers. At this curious moment in musical history the validity of communication in art has itself been called in question, and it is wonderful to have a book where the concentration is entirely on just this, on communication pure and simple. Any and every form of musical style and technique is tried and used: scales, old and new, chords, rhythms, new kinds of instruments—I long to introduce my friend Rostropovich to the one-stringed 'cello, to find out what *he* could do with it. It is indeed salutary to have a description of a composer humbly and un-self-consciously indulging in every sort of freedom, and being guided solely by his success in communicating with, and concern for the well-being of, his young, sick listeners. I can recommend this book wholeheartedly not only to humanitarian readers, but to my musical colleagues as well. We can all learn from it.

B.B.

PREFACE

Autistic or psychotic children and those with severe brain injury are largely cut off from communication with life. There is a poverty of ego, a failure of development of conscious personality, a withdrawal from a world which has proven too painful or a regular misconstruing of signals coming from that world.

Through the methods described in this work, music becomes a non-conflictual entrance into the child's consciousness. The child's own responses participate in an activity which becomes truly creative within a comparatively short time. For the child (and for the observer) this is a tremendously exhilarating experience. There is a gradual awakening response to the personalities of the therapists and here the potentialities of these crippled children are born.

The work of recording the experiences has been done with skill and accuracy. It describes a creative process clearly and understandably, making it available for use for other humanistic musicians in giving active participation in life to otherwise drab existence. It also opens exciting glimpses of new and broadening approaches to further understanding of the human condition.

G. Henry Katz, M.D.,
Senior Psychoanalyst, Lecturer in Psychiatry,
The Institute of the Pennsylvania Hospital

ACKNOWLEDGMENTS

We express our gratitude to:

Herbert Geuter, M.D., Director of Research, Sunfield Children's Homes, for his original research, for giving every opportunity for the development of music therapy, and for the guidance, enthusiasm and collaboration he has so freely given us over the years.

Michael H. Wilson, Director of Sunfield, for his positive response to Nordoff's initial interest in exploring music as therapy with the children at Sunfield; the staff of Sunfield for providing the platform on which our work could begin and for their practical assistance.

G. Henry Katz, M.D., The Institute, Pennsylvania Hospital, whose understanding and wisdom have been invaluable aids in our research.

Bertram A. Ruttenberg, M.D., and Julia Fraknoi, Ph.D., Department of Child Psychiatry, University of Pennsylvania— both indispensable colleagues—and the staff of the Day-Care Unit for autistic children.

Dr and Mrs Martin F. Palmer, Directors, Institute of Logopedics, Wichita, Kansas, who planned our project there and who made our stay particularly fruitful.

Helen C. Bailey, Ph.D., and John B. Taulane, Board of Public Education, Philadelphia, Pa., who inaugurated and supported so wholeheartedly our work as Teacher Consultants in Special Education for the Public Schools of Philadelphia, and the principals and teachers who helped us to carry out this project.

Edward L. French, Ph.D., and J. Clifford Scott, M.D., The Devereux Schools, and Mitchell B. Dratman, M.D., Department of Child Psychiatry, University of Pennsylvania, for their active interest.

Drs Herbert and Gail Levin, music therapists, for their total support in the projects at the Devereux Schools, the University of Pennsylvania, and in the City schools of Philadelphia; Cordelia Livermore for her contribution to the work with autistic children.

Nellie Lee Bok for playing the part in the development of this work that only she could play.

For this edition our thanks go to friends in Germany: Konrad Schily, M.D., and Angela Schily, Gemeinshafts-Krankenhaus, Herdecke, who commissioned the revision of the earlier text; Hanns and Lora Voith, Heidenheim, for their warm assistance; Mechtilde Gräfin Harrach, Munich, for her incomparable hospitality; and Johanna Hirth, Grainau, a staunch, true friend of our work in every way.

SOLALINDEN/PUTZBRUN,
MÜNCHEN,   P.N.
MARCH 1970   C.R.

THERAPY IN MUSIC
FOR
HANDICAPPED CHILDREN

INTRODUCTION

THE THERAPY THAT lies in music can have a far-reaching effect upon the development of children who bear the handicaps of mental impairment, emotional disturbance or physical disability. Over wide ranges of childhood pathology, age, social and economic background, under almost all conditions of special education, institutional or clinical care, this broad assertion holds true.

Music is a universal experience in the sense that all can share in it; its fundamental elements of melody, harmony, and rhythm appeal to, and engage their related psychic functions in each one of us. Music is also universal in that its message, the content of its expression, can encompass all heights and depths of human experience, all shades of feeling. It can lead or accompany the psyche through all conditions of inner experience, whether these be superficial and relatively commonplace or profound and deeply personal.

That the cultural inheritance of music is endowed with countless gifts for every human being is common knowledge, but for those children with whom we are concerned in this book the "gifts" that music holds are so important that they demand our special consideration. Because these children are mentally or emotionally or physically handicapped—or as is very often the case, multiply handicapped—each one is isolated from the course and content of normal human life to a particular extent. Frequently the handicapped child is unable to assimilate life's experiences; he may be confused because he fails to interpret them, he may even misinterpret them. He may have little or no faith in the capacities of his own psyche. His responsiveness to life may be crippled by fear or anxiety; he may live in a vortex of emotion or, conversely, his consciousness can be so remote that it is concerned only with distorted fragments of the realities of existence. Severe physical disability may have confined him from birth, narrowing his developmental contact with life, his communicative difficulties denying him all expectation of competence and fulfilment, his dependency demoralizing him. For children such as these music may become a world of cogent, activating experience.

For the child who is intellectually impaired, music and musical activities can be vivid, intelligible experiences that require no abstract thought. For the emotionally immature or disturbed child the experience of the emotional language of music is inviting: the self-subsistence of its melodies and forms provides security for him. Musical activity can motivate the physically disabled child to use his limbs or voice expressively; its rhythmic-melodic structures then support his activity and induce an order in his control that promotes coordination. Music therefore becomes a sphere of experience, a means of intercommunication and a basis for activity in which handicapped children can find freedom, in varying degrees, from the malfunctions that restrict their lives. As such, music possesses inherent capacities for effecting a uniquely significant contact with handicapped children and for providing an experiential ground for their engagement, their personality development, their integration—both individually and socially. To the extent to which music achieves this it becomes music therapy; in practice, the range of expression of music as an art, and the structural constitution of music as an artistic discipline, are directly involved.

This book will describe how, in adapting to the different conditions and needs of variously handicapped children, music and musically-supported activities become therapeutically effective in many ways. The book is in the nature of a clinical autobiography; our successive projects from 1959 to 1967 are summarized, and stage by stage our experiences with children are described and discussed. Almost all the experiences the children led us into were totally unforeseeable; the depth and intensity of their responses and the directions of their consequent developments have brought us to a new appreciation of the role music can play in the growth and enrichment of children.

It is our purpose in this book to provide an introduction to music therapy with handicapped children which will illustrate the potentiality of its scope and its main musical and psychological perspectives. Our aim is also to provide musicians, therapists, teachers and students with a wide, practical orientation in the implementation of music as therapy by exemplifying the creative use of musical and artistically related principles in a variety of working situations. In both individual and group work numerous techniques are demonstrated. Most descriptions of individual therapy are given in the first person singular for conciseness and in order to reflect the clinical situation.

In attempting to depict the central motivating power of music therapy—*a child's commitment to his musical activity*—we have become all too aware of the limitations of words to describe musical experience. Only music itself can convey the meaning of its experience, and much more is involved in this than auditory stimuli, rhythm, the "tune", associations, and so forth. The statement of music is made moment by moment; what it expresses comes to life as it moves in time. Our experience, as we live with it, is defined by the character and iteration of its structural elements. Our mood is charged by its mood. Our emotions are tempered and held by the changing tensions of its harmony. When we live in the movement of a melody we become identified with it—as children do when they sing it. When we live in the tonal and temporal structures of a musical composition—as children do when they play instruments in it—our participation integrates our responding faculties. It is out of this completeness of the relationship between music and the human being that music therapy in its truest sense arises.

September 1959—June 1960

Sunfield Children's Home, Clent, Stourbridge, Worcestershire.

Residential. 75 children. Ages: 4–17. Pathologies: all children severely subnormal; moderate and severe retardation, mongolism, childhood psychosis, aphasia, multiple handicaps.

This institute sought to promote the social competence and personality development of its patients directly through intensive and varied group activities. The consistent use of a wide range of artistic activities—painting, music, eurythmy, drama and handicrafts—effected an "emotional education" of the children. In order to achieve this aim, care was taken to maintain a high level of quality in these experiences. The effects of this enhancement of consciousness upon the children's behaviour and educability were then channelled into a flexible, resourceful educational programme.

Research in Individual Music Therapy

The openmindedness of the professional staff to the research in music therapy and the absence of any restricted system of psychological thought facilitated a wide perception of the scope of musical influence and the formulation of several working concepts.

In considering the effect of music in individual therapy the research group studied and analysed such components and elements as intervals, consonance-dissonance, rhythms, vibrato, and scaleforms. The practical necessity to apply these freely and experimentally in a clinical setting led to the development of musical improvisation as a basic technique for individual therapy.

The research then concentrated upon the effects of music improvised for severely emotionally disturbed, autistic, and mongoloid children. Eighteen children, a representative cross-section of the population of the Home, received individual music therapy. The focused, clinical use of compositional-improvisational technique formed the essential subject for study throughout except in the cases of two spastic children for whom Herbert Geuter, M.D., the Director of Research, suggested the use of specific musical idioms to accompany particular forms of movement he prescribed for them.

The recording of the working sessions became mandatory for the accurate analysis of individual therapy.

Group Activities

Partly through following the traditions of the Home and partly as a result of research and experimental procedures with over 60 children, several forms of group musical activity were developed:

Pif-Paf-Poltrie: *a working-game.*

The Three Bears: *instrumental playing, songs, rhythmical speech.*

The Elves and the Cobbler: *a play with music to be performed for children with songs for them to sing.*

Children's Play-songs: *especially composed activity-songs.*

I

THE INCEPTION OF THE WORK

GROUP ACTIVITIES

Music structuring and enlivening a special form of game. Natural rhythms of speech in composing songs. The effect of dissonant harmonies upon children's attention, actions and singing.

THE PROJECT BEGAN with Herbert Geuter's suggestion that we collaborate in developing a game for the children based on the story of *Pif-Paf-Poltrie* from Grimm's Fairy Tales.

Working closely with the children, we evolved this simple story into a structured experience for them, combining action, speech, songs and supporting music, with a specific and central task. It became a "working-game", for in the course of it a besom (a birch-twig broom) was made and a mess of leaves, scattered over the floor at the beginning of the game by the teacher, was swept up by the child taking the part of Pif-Paf-Poltrie. The several songs in the game supported and enlivened the action and dialogue. To one of them the children made vigorous and varied rhythmical movements; they marched to another. There was a solo song for Fair Katie to sing as she married Pif-Paf. Sweeping music and a quiet, serious sweeping song accompanied and supported Pif-Paf as he swept. (See photo Appendix II, and also pages 87 to 96.)

In composing songs to dialogue previously spoken by the children the natural rhythms of their speech were always used. The children responded to this and quickly learned melodies composed in this way. For the action songs it was discovered that their movements were best supported by music in which the harmonic element was as active as the tempo and rhythm. The deliberate, judicious use of dissonant harmonies had a liberating effect on the children. Throughout the game, through the dynamic mood of the music, they would awaken to the situation in which they found themselves. The dissonances not only enabled them to march and move with more vigour, but helped them to learn and remember the words and melodies.

Dramatic and musical techniques in creating a play to be performed for children. Songs form the play's structure and increase participation. The possibilities of dramatic build-up in repeating an established play-structure. Development of mood. Effects of increasing instrumentation.

During November and December, in preparation for Christmas, we composed a play with music to be performed by the staff for the children. In doing this we were following the Home's traditional celebration of Advent. The play was in four episodes, one for each Advent Sunday, and was so written and produced that the dramatic content grew from week to week, reaching its climax on the Sunday preceding Christmas. The story chosen was *The Elves and the Cobbler* from Grimm. In dramatizing it we endeavoured to keep the action, the songs, and the dialogue within the range of the children's understanding, while retaining all the warmth and delight of the story.

To give character to the various scenes in the play and to make them memorable, eight songs were written, each accompanying a particular piece of stage action or expressing a dramatic mood. The singing of six of these, completely or in part, by the children in the audience drew them into the play. Because of the repetitive structure of the story, the same basic sequence—the Wife cleans the house; the Cobbler cuts out leather for shoes; both go to bed; the Elves appear, make the shoes and disappear; the old couple get up, eat breakfast, discover the shoes, and are delighted and grateful when wealthy people buy them—this sequence, every scene of which was supported by a song, could underlie each Sunday's performance. It established a musical-dramatic structure into which, as the story unfolded, each episode's new developments could be introduced; as, for example, when two pairs of shoes were made, and then four pairs, and the number of singing, waltzing customers correspondingly increased, or when, on the third Sunday, the Cobbler and his wife stayed up, hid and saw the Elves at work. On the basis of what was already familiar in scene, sequence and song the children could assimilate the new extensions of the action, absorb their meaning and enjoy them. Similarly, the reversal of action in the fourth episode when the old couple made clothes for the Elves to find and then to wear, was dramatically both surprising and comprehensible. The same sequence could also carry a different mood in each episode as the fortunes of the Cobbler and his wife changed. The mood, tinged with sadness and resignation on the first Sunday, brightened each week, moving through happy thoughtfulness to wonder, then amazement, and finally to warm joy. The stability of the dramatic structure facilitated the children's experience of the play's evolving emotional content.

The piano was placed in the auditorium, actually in the audience itself. Week by week, as the children followed the plot with more comprehension and sang the songs with more feeling for their meaning, both these experiences were augmented by adding other instruments to the piano—first a violin and 'cello, then a drum, and finally a flute and glockenspiel. Thus, an ever richer musical experience intensified the children's growing dramatic involvement.

These methods of production enabled the children to enter into a vivid experiencing of the play. The songs and all they were associated with became part of their daily life in the Home; for months afterwards they were singing and acting them.

Exploration of instrumental activities for handicapped children. An experimentally developed musical setting and dramatic structure heightens the effectiveness of simple instrumental activities. Instrumental variety. Instrumental parts in songs. Antiphony in singing and rhythmical speech to stimulate verbally handicapped children. More capable children demonstrate a musical structure to those less capable. Functional discipline in structured instrumental activities.

In January 1960, we began to work intensively on an experiment with musical instruments that we had started two months previously. In trying to find a way to give children with limited abilities a group musical experience in which they could participate as performers, we had been experimenting with the most elementary means of producing musical tones of good quality.

We had hit upon using a 'cello with one string and two violins, each with one string. These were so tuned that a mildly dissonant chord, encompassing two octaves and a sixth, sounded when they played together. Children learned to bow the strings in the open position, their playing being led and structured by improvised rhythmical speech accompanied by improvised music. The idea of a musical composition using several simple instruments began to take shape. The three string instruments very naturally suggested the story of *The Three Bears*. Working with the children and guided by their abilities, we began to write songs and speech passages with parts for a variety of simple instruments. A number of bird-calls were found that the children could use; played in a song these became birds in the forest. A lyre was chosen to be Goldilocks, and a small harp, her shadow; a song was composed in which the musical motives played by Goldilocks were imitated by the shadow. Drums, a horn and a cymbal were added in other songs as the work progressed. At a dramatic point in the story a bell (Mother Bear's breakfast bell) had to be rung. This became an important part for a child too handicapped to play an instrument. In all, eight songs were written for the children to sing. Singing and rhythmical speech were also used antiphonally to stimulate the children's speech, for many were only partially verbal. Finally, the instrumental parts the children had learned to play were composed into an Overture. What they had learned to do with the aid of words they now performed to music alone. The experiment begun four months earlier became a work for an orchestra of sixteen children who played specific parts in special musical contexts. The complete work lasted twenty-five minutes. It was performed for the parents at Easter, 1960, and again a month later for a group of doctors, psychiatrists, and psychiatric social workers from the Midland Nerve Hospital, Birmingham. (Photos Appendix II.)

The performances gave the children great pleasure and they experienced the satisfaction and confidence that accomplishment gives. The work proved to be beneficial not only to the sixteen children in the orchestra, but also to the forty or fifty who sat and sang in the audience. All the children, even the most retarded, were eager to perform it. For most, to learn the instrumental parts, simple though they were, required an all-out effort. But their enthusiasm carried them along, and almost without realizing it they accepted the high degree of discipline that playing in *The Three Bears* entailed. Because of this, the sections of the work were used selectively with smaller groups to help children develop concentration, self-control and increased self and social awareness.

The development of songs to increase awareness and social interaction.

The children's response to the music and songs that were being composed for them and the ease with which they were learning and remembering songs indicated that these could be used for quite specific purposes. We were working with children whose conceptual abilities were necessarily limited. Many of them found it difficult to form associations with the world beyond those that related them to the most basic elements of their daily life.

We composed a number of songs designed to help the children to a greater awareness. These were used at first in the group settings; often a single child was encouraged to sing a solo part and perform its actions while the other children in the class sang responses and choruses. Among the songs there was one about the weather, another about colours and counting —in which buttons were counted on the "grey" shirt or the "red" dress. There was a song in which the child was encouraged to spell his name, another about the days of the week, yet another about a house. Others were composed to be sufficiently flexible to include any subject that the teacher might wish to bring to the children. These came to be called *Playsongs*.

Different forms of musical activity become features of a developmental social environment.

These varied types of group activity demonstrated to us how specially composed music could be used to enliven and extend the personal, social and educational experiences of retarded children. Working with the experiential qualities music could communicate we saw that their lives could be enriched and they could get more out of their experiences as individuals, and as members of a group.

The Elves and the Cobbler, Pif-Paf-Poltrie, the instrumental activity and the songs filled the Home with music; much of it had been composed or evolved in classroom work out of situations that could be structured or given an enhanced meaning by a song. *Pif-Paf* helped many children to experience for the first time the integration and steadfastness necessary for doing a difficult job well and seeing it through. *The Three Bears* gave each participating child rich musical stimulation and the experience of working purposefully with others to perform an ordered composition. The *Play-songs* sung solo, antiphonally, or in unison led many children to attain a more active and conscious awareness of the subject they sang about, and also to share their pleasure in it.

INDIVIDUAL THERAPY

During the entire project, explorative work shaped the development of individual therapy.

Music organizes and intensifies a movement exercise and increases its effect.

For one hypertonic epileptic boy, Dr Geuter had prescribed a specific movement. Although this boy could take only small awkward steps and was unable to raise his arms above his shoulders, the goal of the exercise was to get him to take a big stride and at the same time thrust his arms outwards, spreading them above his head. He was to attempt to make this large free movement by his own efforts to a definite rhythm, one often found in Spanish music. The eurythmist was to encourage and lead him. It was recommended that the exercise be supported by music. After seven months, having worked thrice weekly, he was able to perform it successfully. As a result all his movements became freer and the tensions that had hindered his mixing with others began to ease. His speech became less strained and gained in fluency. The strongly accented accompaniment in the Spanish idiom I used was an essential part of the treatment.

Improvisation used to contact a remote, unresponsive child. The characters of musical idioms become important.

Dr Geuter suggested that music be played for a five-year-old regressed, psychotic child and his responses observed.

In the first session I found through improvising in several idioms that he reacted very differently to music in two widely disparate scale forms. When this was discussed with the staff it was agreed that as there was virtually nothing that could be done for the boy other than sedation, this sensitivity to music offered a means of reaching him that should be followed up. Subsequently, he had individual music sessions over a period of eight months. During this time his receptiveness to music steadily increased and he became less remote. The change in his mood as his behaviour relaxed called for the intensification of his music. A succession of specific musical-emotional experiences—based on pentatonic, modal and major scales—evolved, to which he responded so calmly and positively that a definite improvement in his condition was evident.

Using the modal scale in which much of his music had been improvised, I composed simple music to be played on a lyre for him each night at bedtime. It was noticed that when for some unavoidable reason this could not be played for him he slept badly.

Rhythmically chaotic drum-beating as expressive of lack of integration. Improvisation used to engage a child and bring order into his activity.

Later in the project, to supplement a study being made by the staff of a nine-year-old mongol boy, Dr Geuter requested a musical investigation.

The boy was sat at the treble end of the keyboard to see how he would react to my playing. The result was entirely unexpected. As he tapped the piano keys this severely retarded boy with extremely limited intellectual possibilities and very little speech, revealed that a dynamic source of complex rhythmic impulses lived within him. In response to the improvisation he would play impulsive rhythmic patterns and intricate syncopations. His "music" was free, playful, and completely unpredictable, yet it bore a fragmented rhythmic structure that was related to the improvisation.

Following the investigatory session, rhythmic work was begun with the boy with a side drum (without snare) and an attached cymbal; he used a pair of sticks or brushes to beat his rhythmic reaction to the lively music I played. Sometimes he would follow me briefly, at other times I would follow him, adapting my improvisation to his beating. This was exuberant and creative; he would change tempi and dynamics, using the drum and cymbal in a way that could not be foreseen, yet which was often artistically "right", musically effective, and sometimes surprisingly beautiful.

He seemed to be at that stage of inner chaos where creative freedom merges into incomprehensibility and incoherence. The drum-beating was not at first a consciously self-directed activity for this boy. He was utterly absorbed in realizing expression of the rhythmic impulses that lived within him. Consciousness of what he was doing developed later in the sessions as he experienced his beating impulses being answered in the music that surrounded him. When this happened, and the boy and I really met in the music, the activity that had been a playful and unpredictable game began to take on the form of a musical give-and-take. From this his beating gradually became more ordered; for longer periods he would beat the basic beat of the improvisations, and he began to try to beat the melodic rhythms of *Play-songs* he knew. This required a concentrated effort from him—in his musical activities and experiences he had begun to form faculties that he was now using directedly for the first time.

Towards the end of the work one of the teachers noticed a change in the boy. In his daily life he seemed generally more awake and purposeful. This happened over a period of six weeks during which he had had fifteen music sessions. (See also page 72, photos Appendix I, 4.)

It was exciting to find that through the medium of the drum this boy expressed inner qualities and a developmental condition which would otherwise have remained undetected. Also, his response which would have seemed meaningless and arbitrary to a layman's ear, could be perceived by a musician to be subtle compounds of rhythms.

* * *

All the children we worked with were pleased to beat the drum to the piano and it was obvious that they felt the innate pleasure almost everyone does in rhythmic expression. Several other children revealed their own rhythmic pictures.

Compulsive beating as symptomatic of lack of contact. A simple melodic-rhythmic pattern induces a controlled response. Melodic form extends vocal activity. First developments in speech formation emerge in singing.

A young, speechless, hyperactive girl could beat only a very slow, compulsive beat. This would remain in its regular metronomic tempo, no matter what music was played. Her restricted ability to relate to life expressed itself musically as an unawareness of the most basic element of music. Eventually, by using a counter-rhythm—two beats against three—in working with her beating, I was able to "break" her fixed beat; she speeded up her tempo and beat with the improvisation. She retained and gradually extended this freedom. At about the same time, in response to group activity, she began to "speak" the repeating rhythmic phrase from the song "Pif-Paf-Poltrie and Fair Katie", at first rhythmically uttering the vowels and then approximating the words. Later, from speaking it, she began to sing it and by degrees her enunciation improved. Within two months she went on to sing other songs whose melodic quality was more lyric than rhythmic. One of these was

"Something is Going to Happen",* the thoughtful song that introduced *The Elves and the Cobbler*. She derived great pleasure from this, and it was obvious that she was drawn to the expressiveness and order of melody. The music classes now became a social experience for her; this also was a new event in her development. Subsequently she learned to speak.

Looking back, one has the feeling that this girl needed to experience the world of melody. A melody is an entity existing in time—an expressive human experience occurring in time. Her relationship to time was originally fragmentary and disordered: in the melodies she grew to love, she found a secure stable element; she entered the world of melody through the gateway of rhythm.

The security of the basic beat supports the joy of active freedom. Fear is overcome by musical pleasure.

A lightly-built mongol boy who appeared aware of far more than he could bring himself to do was too frightened to beat the drum at first. Eventually, with the example of other children happily beating with me, he began to beat. His initial beating was fixed, fast and light, and it was impossible to bring him to beat with the improvisations. It was as if some deeply seated fear or nervousness prevented him from making any close relationship even in the music.

After a time, I was able to get him to beat tentatively to some songs he knew from *Pif-Paf-Poltrie* and *The Elves and the Cobbler*. One of these, "The Shoe Making Song",* is rather quick and has many rests in the music. When these occur, they do so on the second beat in the measure. He began beating to the song and almost immediately found that he had beaten through a rest. He was startled that he had beaten the drum alone, but as we played together on the next beat and the song

* Nordoff and Robbins, *The First Book of Children's Play-Songs*, Theodore Presser Co., 1961.

carried us onward, some confidence returned. The recurring rests continued to trouble him, and for a while he was worried. Then he discovered a wonderful thing. He found that the basic pulse of the song could support him as he beat through the rests. This realization, born out of an active musical experience, gave him courage and he continued to beat the basic beat squarely through the rests, flashing me looks of daring and delight as he did so. He experienced the feeling of making music together with me, and found great pleasure in expressing himself at last, secure upon the completely dependable foundation of the basic beat of music.

* * *

The children at Sunfield were demonstrating that for them music was a vivid and many-featured world. If their involvement was to be correctly understood, the elements of music would have to be carefully and imaginatively considered. It was obvious from the children's pleasure that they derived deep satisfaction from their musical experiences. One could not avoid the feeling that experiences as deep and as joyful as these, which at the same time called for the total participation of the individual, must be therapeutic.

Working individually with the drum in a group setting. Children lead each other into closer musical attention. They disclose unsuspected musical perceptiveness.

The drum and the cymbal became such an attraction for the children that we began to use them in the group activities. One by one the children would come to the drum and beat with the music while the rest of the class sat and watched, listening intently. One or two were so well-organized that they would sense the final cadence in the improvisation or song, and intuitively use the cymbal for the final beat. Observing this, other children would get the idea and try to do this when their turn came; they would have to be awake, attentive to the music, and sufficiently in control of their beating to hit the cymbal at the right moment. This was difficult for many, but they tried hard. Success meant a round of applause and that pleasurable feeling of accomplishment. The children began to teach themselves the rudiments of musical structure.

The children spontaneously used the drum and cymbal in other ways. Two of the most retarded mongoloid boys in the Home would beat *Play-songs* they knew, using the cymbal for one phrase, the drum for another. The way they did this revealed an intensity of experience we had not suspected, and a creativity that was astonishing. The cymbal also possessed the virtue of being stimulating. One boy who was usually apathetic and inactive would become intensely awake when he beat the cymbal. He would play fortissimo for long periods to supporting music.

An effect of instrumental timbre. Children's individual affinity with particular tonal qualities.

There were a few children for whom the drum proved unsuitable, and for them other instruments were used. One lethargic girl became vivacious and animated when she strummed a small guitar to the rhythm of an improvisation. She enjoyed the dry quality of this instrument's sound. A boy who had had a definite distaste for music when he entered the Home, became fascinated by the toy harp that was used in *The Three Bears*. It had a rather thin, delicate sound. He would play *glissandi* and listen to them with pleasure. Before the project finished, he was able to play a simple melodic phrase from "Pif-Paf-Poltrie's March" on the harp.

A seven-year-old delicate mongoloid boy found quiet satisfaction in striking a number of small Indian bells hung from a little tree. He struck them singly with care and would occasionally shake the entire tree gently to sound a brilliant peal of bells. The accompanying music, improvised in the oriental scale made by the bell tones, was played mostly in the treble over pedal points. The mood of its idiomatic character with the sound of the bell tones, created a tonal-emotional environment in which his absorbed playing assumed an intense expressive substantiality. (Photos Appendix I, 2.)

In their individual character, children's musical responses are descriptive of their psychological and developmental condition. Both progressive attributes and pathological factors are revealed. Forms of musical response hold diagnostic implications.

These explorations disclosed that each child reacted differently to music. Many expressed their individuality or state of development in their relationship to a specific element of music. One child would be engaged in assimilating the element of structure, another lived in the melodic element, while yet another found security in the basic beat. Some children, on the whole those less organized and more handicapped, would be strongly affected by musical idioms. The style and mood of the music that was played evoked important responses from them. Empirical work led to the improvising of Oriental music, medieval church music, eastern European music, and other styles with different geographical and historical origins. The most romantic music was needed by one boy, while yet another required the most dissonant.

The children were making musical "self-portraits" in the way they were reacting to music thus improvised. Each was different, and it was becoming evident that there must be a direct connection between an individual's pathology, his personality, and the musical self-portrait he revealed; that the reaction to music in each case could be descriptive of the psychological condition. If one could learn to interpret it adequately, the way a child lived in the world of music could be taken as an aid to diagnosis, as a help in assessing his needs and potentialities.

* * *

This was as far as music therapy with groups and individuals could progress at Sunfield, for in June the time came to leave. It was with regret that we had to discontinue the work, and we were sorry to leave the many friends we had made among the children. But above all we felt strongly challenged to explore further and to find our way about this new world of music therapy into which they had led us.

June—November 1960

European Tour
Visits made to 24 institutes for handicapped children in England, Scotland, Sweden, Denmark, Holland, Germany and Switzerland. Demonstrations of individual therapy with children of various nationalities. New techniques emerge. Pif-Paf-Poltrie and other group activities demonstrated; translations made for many institutes.

II

THE WIDENING EXPLORATION

THE PURPOSE OF the European tour was originally to gain comparative experience of various educational and residential centres. We were interested in the different ways of life they offered children, in the general and special features of their programmes and in their use of the arts in therapy, particularly music, and music with movement or drama. Twenty of the institutes we visited were "Steiner Homes", so called because of their adherence to principles of educational therapy developed by Rudolf Steiner during the first quarter of the century. The pioneering experimentation in the application of art forms to therapy in this movement had resulted in treatment practices we wanted to observe.

A detailed report of our impressions is beyond the scope of this book. What was good was inspiringly good: at Jarna, near Stockholm, architectural form and colour combined in school and residential buildings to create a therapeutic environment for disturbed children; in Bristol, England and Heidenheim, Germany, there was the effective use of music, pageant and drama; in Bingenheim, Germany, the engaging, disciplined movement of eurythmy; at Bieldside, Aberdeenshire, creative speech therapy; at St Barthelemy, Switzerland, imaginative puppetry; there were models of community living for children in West Linton, Scotland and Holte, near Copenhagen, and for young adults at Oploo, Holland. At Sunfield we had previously seen the use of designed images in projected colour and painting therapies. These were the highlights of our experiences; the purposefulness of the human and artistic care we saw applied, reinforced our own feelings about the realization of therapy.

* * *

Throughout the tour we were able to take our investigations in music therapy further; for, from the beginning, the visits took the form of an exchange. After being shown aspects of the life of an institution we would be asked to describe our work. As the best description was live demonstration, wherever it was possible we worked with children.

A concise method of introducing *Pif-Paf-Poltrie* evolved and we were able to demonstrate it with children in thirteen institutes. In Denmark, Holland and Germany, translations were made. At every demonstration children responded as had those at Sunfield. In Holland, where we had to lead the game through an interpreter holding a translation (the ink was still wet), it made the same impact. We were increasingly impressed with the fact that in giving us this deceptively simple dialogue to turn into a game, Herbert Geuter had indeed recognized a theme with a universal meaning for children.

The Three Bears was taught in its entirety to adolescent children in Scotland, and sections were used with variously handicapped children in several institutes. *Play-songs* were used in English or in translation in most places.

In describing individual therapy we occasionally made use of tape-recordings made at Sunfield. These became a useful means of illustrating children's responses and the necessity for improvisation. In six institutes individual therapy was demonstrated directly with children. This resulted in new principles of the therapy becoming evident.

Dissonant, dramatic music engages psychotic children. Communication begins by matching a child's inner condition with music.

During the three weeks we were at the Camphill Rudolf Steiner Schools in Scotland, we worked on three occasions with a number of eight- to ten-year-old psychotic children. The limited time rendered the demonstrations inconclusive as therapy. One fact, however, emerged: dynamic, dissonant music does not necessarily excite or disturb psychotic children.

Children who were usually distractable, hyperactive and difficult to manage, sat quietly in the sessions listening to each other's work on the drum. As I aimed to express the turbulence of their emotional lives in the music I improvised, it was often wild and dissonant. This experience appeared to be more significant for them than quiet, soothing music which might have been considered more suitable.

I had the feeling that music therapy in this situation could not consist in using music as a tranquillizer. The music therapist would have to take hold of the child's disordered life of impulse as it expressed itself rhythmically and work with this musically. Therapy would then lie in leading the child into the experiences of mobility and organization latent in the world of music. The child could only accompany me into this world and gain these experiences through his own activity. Together we had to begin where he was, at that level of communication determined by his pathology and revealed in his drum-beating. While some children beat spontaneously and openly, others, afraid of the turmoil that lived within them, would ask continually for simple, rhythmical songs. They would beat to these mechanically and unfeelingly, using the songs as a screen to reinforce their autism. Only by working with the disorder that lies behind such behaviour could one hope to achieve any fundamental therapy.

Individuality of response demonstrated by Educationally Subnormal children. Musical communication by-passes the language barrier.

At Villa Marjatta in Denmark, demonstrations were given with about twenty children; there was only time to take each child once. These children were not as ill as the psychotic children described above nor as heavily retarded as those at Sunfield. Their reactions were very telling. The members of the staff observing these sessions were impressed by the immediacy with which the children entered completely into the activity of beating the drum to piano improvisations. This was all the more impressive as there could be no contact through language: communication between each child and the pianist was necessarily entirely musical.

As one after the other the children came to beat the drum, the differences in their personalities and pathologies were clearly shown. A spastic boy showed his acuity in his perception of rhythmic patterns; his determination to express this was apparent in his struggle to master impaired muscular coordination. An autistic boy with a high degree of organization revealed his pathology by beating compulsively in a tempo having no relation to the unfamiliar music played for him. A girl with a limited scholastic potential showed sensitivity and intelligence in the way she used drum and cymbal to enhance the music. A lively retarded boy revealed a fiery creative ability which he could neither sustain nor develop. His reaction to the improvisation soon exposed the lack of organization that was hindering his performance, robbing him of self-confidence.

The different responses of all the children demonstrated to the staff how different individual music therapy would have to be for each one.

Significant musical contact with an autistic, retarded young man. Clinical control of tension and relaxation through improvisation.

Among the institutes we visited in Holland was a home for older boys and young men. The patients and staff were engaged in farming, gardening, crafts and household occupations. The tranquillity and humanity of the community life impressed us deeply.

Following the lecture we gave on our first evening, a teacher approached us and asked if we would work with her son, a patient in the home. The boy was eighteen, mentally handicapped and autistic. Often in the past he had shown a tense, spasmodical reaction to music. His mother felt that this way of using music could be important for him.

The next morning the boy was given an exploratory session. His response was positive; it indicated musical sensitivity, although he was somewhat inhibited by the presence of both parents. I asked to take him alone in the afternoon and this time discovered that he reacted strongly to a certain kind of dissonant music. As he became aroused he put considerable effort into beating the basic beat—as the music became more dissonant and forceful, he became increasingly animated. It was clear that we were reaching forces within him that were usually dormant, unfamiliar to him. He was stirred and excited both by the music itself and by being at one with it through the vigour of his own response. Then we reached a moment when he began to lose control; his excitement passed into bewilderment as his own vitality threatened to overwhelm him. His beating began to be frantic. Seeing this I changed the music, introducing a quiet melody composed of short phrases based on a triplet rhythm, using mainly one dissonant and two perfect intervals. This relaxed him so quickly that he was soon beating the melodic rhythm with considerable consciousness and pleasure.

The quieter music was meaningfully experienced by the boy because it had been preceded by the extreme tension of the dissonances and syncopations which had aroused his inherent vitality. Limited by his pathology, he had never learned to exercise this innate vitality; when it was now aroused by stimulating music it threatened to overpower him. Therapy for this boy would lie in leading him towards making his forces his own through giving him opportunities to order his organic and emotional reactions himself. I felt intuitively that active participation in specific musical experiences could achieve this. It would mean working with music as vital and mobile as the human forces involved, while using a principle of tension and relaxation always carefully adjusted to the boy's reactions. It would be a powerful therapy, one not lightly to be undertaken, but it was clear that the boy needed it. His age, his secure relationship with his parents, and the overall warmth of the life of the home would support him.

As we were leaving the next day, and the boy was eager to repeat his musical experiences, he was given another session later in the afternoon and one the following morning. In both I worked with the principle of tension and relaxation using the calm triplet motif as a secure, stable element to which I could return whenever necessary. He made progress in these sessions; as his drum-beating became more organized and purposeful his self-control increased. As these experiences were so obviously significant for him, enough of the improvised music was written out to enable his mother to continue the work.

Discussions concerning therapeutic approach and musical freedom: dissonance, an essential and expressive harmonic component; drumbeating as a means of communication. Ego-activity in music therapy.

The visits to Sonnenhof, Switzerland and Bingenheim, Germany were important because of the clarification of concepts our experiences there demanded. Both institutes placed great value on music in the lives of their children and in the discussions that took place we were seriously challenged to justify our use of music. Many workers found much of it too loud, too dissonant and too rhythmic. They were of the opinion that music for handicapped children should be soothing, rather soft, conventionally harmonious, and, if active, not stimulating.

It was necessary to make a clear distinction between a child's passive and active experience of music. We had several times seen music used as a pleasant pastime in which adults and children sat together listening; occasionally children would be gently encouraged to sing or to tap a triangle in a rather indiscriminate way. Doubtless some therapeutic benefits could accrue from the possible soothing effects of listening in an undemanding social atmosphere and from this unchallenging kind of participation. But this was more a mild form of entertainment than a music therapy, and could become a subduing, conditioning factor in a child's life. Music, we fervently believed, could be more than this.

We were asked why dissonance was used so freely in both improvisations and songs composed for the children. We pointed out that dissonance is not an innovation of the contemporary composer. It is essential to the structure of eighteenth-century music; the development of the expressive use of dissonance is integral to the music of the nineteenth century. But we are all so familiar with this music that we do not readily perceive its dissonances as being "dissonant", and so do not react negatively to them. The dissonances in the harmonic developments of the present century are still too new or confusing for many people, who therefore find it hard to discriminate between different *degrees* of dissonance. The degree—and quality—of dissonance in a harmony is an essential component of its expressive content. It is a vital factor in enlivening and sustaining the flow of music in time. In therapy we had never had the experience that dissonances used appropriately disturb or harm handicapped children. On the contrary, expressive dissonance helps to awaken them to the musical activity in which they are engaged. Dissonances can set a child into movement, can increase his attention-span, and can give vitality to the harmonic accompaniment of the songs he sings. As the dissonance is a fundamental element of music it must be capable of being used therapeutically.

We also had to justify the use of the drum, for we encountered a prejudice against drum-beating: it was held to be a primitive, barbaric activity capable of expressing only blind or obsessive impulses of a low order. We explained that the rhythmical coactivity of a child and therapist in an improvisation could take the child into experiences full of subtlety and refinement. The child's musical recognition of the elements of his experience and his spontaneous response—expressed through the drum—would then constitute a qualitative communication of a very high order.

We were invited to work with children at both institutes. This went well, the children demonstrated how much music in its mobility could mean to them. This was intently observed by our friendly protagonists. At Bingenheim, Dr Gotthard Starke became interested and suggested that we stay to develop the therapy further with his children. This was encouraging but our impending departure for the United States made acceptance impossible. Dr Helmut Klimm of Sonnenhof watched a number of his boys working hard in individual therapy, ordering and freeing their responses despite autism, compulsions, and impairments. At the conclusion of the work he said, "In most of our activity we surround the child and work from the periphery. In this use of music the ego is taken hold of directly and brought into activity within the impaired or disturbed emotional life."

* * *

In the children's responses to the materials which were demonstrated, and to the improvisational techniques that were evolving, we found inspiring confirmation; we could not help but feel them to be partners in a very living form of music therapy research.

February—July 1961

The Devereux Schools, Devon, Pennsylvania.
*Residential. Pathologies: childhood schizophrenia, emotional
disturbance, autism, brain-injury, retardation. Ages: 5–14.
Fifteen children received individual music therapy; 208
individual sessions given. Thirty children participated in
group musical activities.*

Research in Individual Therapy
*The further development of therapeutic techniques yielded a
considerable amount of research data classified under the following
headings:*
Musical idiom.
Emotional, perceptual and ideational effects of tempo.
Give-and-take in musical activities.
Vocal responses and creative singing.
Freeing a child from "singing echolalia".
Introduction of learning situations.
Development of specific use of songs for individuals.
Breaking compulsive beating tempi.
*Breaking down of monotone singing to yield greater verbal and
vocal freedom.*
Rhythmic patterns.
*Use of specific rhythmic work on drum and cymbal to overcome
physical rigidities and their psychological accompaniments.*

Group Activities
Pif-Paf-Poltrie *used with two groups. Several new* Play-songs
developed.

47

Conducted concurrently, a pilot project at the Day-Care Unit, Department of Child Psychiatry, School of Medicine, University of Pennsylvania.

Pathologies: childhood psychosis, severe autism, symbiosis. Ages 2½–8. The 15 children attending the unit all received individual therapy. 167 sessions given.

Research

Detailed analysis of each child's musical responses and a concentration on the development of improvisational techniques to bring about involvement, communication and relationship. Of special importance were:

Clinical control of emotional responses to musical stimuli.

Changing a child's prevailing mood.

Modifying behaviour patterns through musical experience.

Development of clinical vocal techniques.

Freeing a child from evasive behaviour.

Influence of scale tonality upon a child's crying.

Emerging speech in therapy sessions.

Pathological manifestations in the child's way of beating.

Implications of overall response to music therapy in differential diagnosis.

* * *

Both these projects added considerably to our experiences in individual therapy, confirming much that had previously been effected while bringing in many new kinds of response and new modes of therapeutic activity. Yet all was related; similar principles of approach, response and development ran through the diverse clinical phenomena we recorded. To organize our considerations and to arrive at a rationale of the practice and processes of individual therapy, the following statement was prepared.

III

OUTLINE OF A NEW MUSIC THERAPY

*The word "exceptional" is not used here to denote that which
is superior or above the average. It is used in its meaning of
"unusual, not following the rule". This meaning carries an
implication of exclusion. All children who live within the
conditions imposed upon them by an organic or emotional
pathology lead exceptional lives in this sense.*

MUSIC IS A universal means of communication. It has been
called a non-verbal language. What has yet to be more clearly
recognized is the range of expression that is possible in this
"language". The variety of human expression that can be
communicated through music is highly diversified and virtually
unlimited. Because of this, music becomes vitally important as
therapy for exceptional children.

Music is essentially an emotional experience and can be as
wide and varied in its content as the human emotions themselves. Fundamentally, the way a person feels is more important
to his life and development than the way he thinks. Feelings
are of primary importance to children. A happy child is happy
because he spontaneously feels happy, not because he knows
what happiness is. A child may be able to think clearly, to learn
well, but it is what he feels about what he knows that determines
what he does with his knowledge and its ultimate value to himself and the world. The learning process itself is entirely subject to the child's feelings towards the object of study. Not only
is his thinking dependent upon his emotional life but the
motivation and activation of his will are directly involved.

49

Children do not do anything well unless they want to do it. Want is an emotional condition. The way a child goes about an action is a function of the way he feels about it. If the emotional life is impulsive, or unstable, or torpid, the behaviour will possess the same characteristics.

The emotional life of a child is reached directly by music. If he sits in a chair listening to music his experiences may be vivid or dreamy depending upon his character and, not less, upon the character of the music. But if he stands at a drum, is given sticks and asked to beat to the music, then immediately, as he becomes active, he becomes directly, personally involved in rhythmic activity and in musical experience. When the music consists of piano improvisations in different musical styles and the child follows each change in the music as it occurs, he is listening, alert, and controlling what he is doing. As the structural elements of melody and harmony are repeated and developed, he can recognize these and anticipate *crescendi*, changes of tempi, cadences or other components. The music is in movement—the child's emotional experiences are also in movement. The improvisations can be sombre in character or they can be humorous, they can be stirring or gay, or tender or elevating. These adjectives refer to emotions; as the child becomes actively engaged in such music he experiences its emotional content closely. Living in the emotional character of the music, recognizing the elements of structure on which it is formed, and expressing his responses freely in his beating, he has an important experience: his whole personality is vividly activated and working harmoniously.

A child who can do these things has reached a fairly high level of musical participation, probably attainable by most eight- or nine-year-olds. There are higher levels which involve other uses of the drum than beating the basic beat—such as the beating of the rhythms of melodies, the accompanying of the improvisation with rhythmic patterns, or the controlled use of drum and cymbal to punctuate the structure or to heighten the play of dynamics. A still higher level is reached when the child becomes creative and freely uses these rhythmic possibilities and others of his own invention. On this level he is not only receiving an experience, he is participating in its realization. At the creative moment he feels with intuitive certainty the quality his activity must have and the expressive form it must take in the on-going experience. Spontaneously, he perceives an artistic "necessity" and becomes creative.

Wonderful things happen to a child who achieves this: the vital life of feeling becomes united with perceiving, with intelligent comprehension and with action—and all are integrated by the essential individuality of the child in communicative expressiveness.

To offer this world of potential experience to an exceptional child is to offer him the opportunity to bring the different elements of his being into function and synthesis in a uniquely significant way. The innate or developmental anomalies that have rendered the child exceptional also determine the way in which he responds to musical experience. This becomes apparent very quickly when he beats a drum to piano improvisations. To whatever he beats, music is improvised. He will react to this and the nature of his reaction will determine how the improvisation proceeds. The improvisation has a searching character and in the space of a few minutes the child will have presented a musical-rhythmic picture of himself.

He will have shown whether he is rhythmically free, whether he is creative, or if his rhythmic expression is hindered. His drum-beating may be mechanical and not musical. He may be able to beat in different tempi but become fixed in them once they are established. His beating may even be compulsive, in one fixed tempo that he is unable to relate to the music. It may consist of compulsive repetitive rhythmic patterns or tremors. Disorganized beating may also intervene in the experience that the music offers.

These and other rhythmic responses are to be found among

exceptional children. Although the responses of children of similar pathologies may resemble each other the musical self-portrait is highly individualized. No two children react exactly alike and responses can never be predicted.

The forms of the rhythmic responses are of neurological and psychological interest because of the relationship they can bear to the vital rhythms of the organism and to both central and peripheral nervous system functions. The complex relationship between the operation of the organism and the emotional life is immediately relevant, particularly where an emotional disturbance coexists with a known physical impairment.

Children's first responses to the therapy situation are often impressive. If a child is unable to relate his beating to the music the therapist relates the improvisation to whatever the child is doing; he is then usually able to make a tentative relationship to the music. Frequently, apathetic children become surprisingly vigorous. The drum and cymbal are inherently attractive to children, and those who do not readily communicate in other ways often express themselves strongly upon them. Whatever they beat is met musically and developed by the therapist. As the interaction is within the order of musical structure the character and extent of the children's activities can be accurately described in musical terms. Many who score a low I.Q. can show, in their musical responses, perception, intelligence, and other inherent capacities which throw new light on their potential.

Psychologists are interested in the investigational possibilities of improvised music therapy for it evidences qualities in a child that do not readily show up in standard tests. Psychiatrists see the therapy as arousing children's enthusiasm, developing mastery and the sense of goal-attainment, and providing a direct means of stimulating a child to communicate and relate to people and the world around him.

In subsequent sessions most children take up their musical-emotional experiences with a deepened interest and purpose.

In so doing they enter a new world of experience, of order, of expression. Those with a relatively light impairment or slight emotional disturbance are on the threshold of this world. It may be that they become free to enter it as they overcome some compulsive tendencies in their beating. Many begin by beating the basic beat and find their confidence in this before proceeding further. Some will order a compulsive beat by beating the rhythm of a melody or a rhythmic pattern until they discover the basic beat. Others begin by beating an unpredictable rhythmic chaos that would be potentially creative if it did not lack the structure and stability upon which creativity takes form and meaning. These children order their being as they order their beating, realizing order and purpose in themselves as they find these qualities in the music.

Whatever form the child's entry into this world takes, all its possibilities for stimulation and growth surround him once he is active in it. The rate of his progress will depend upon the extent of his pathology, his age, his personality, and the environmental conditions in which he lives. It will also depend upon the musicianship, insight, and attitude of the therapists and the amount of energy and time they can give him. It has been demonstrated that significant experiences within the therapy sessions begin to play comparatively soon into the child's total life. In some cases the effects are striking and easily noticed while in others the results need a more subtle perception to be truly evaluated.

The character of the music that mediates these experiences is the groundwork of the therapy; the way it is used by the musician mediates the therapeutic process itself. The living, dynamic elements of music draw the child into activity; his interest is held throughout the session by the constant relationship that is maintained between his responsiveness and the music through the form the improvisation takes.

The more capable children need a wide range of musical experiences; improvisations for them include music that is romantic, dramatic, lyric, dance-like, and symphonic. Less advanced children may respond only to one of these idioms, the emotional quality and structural characteristics of a particular idiom being of especial significance to them. Many react strongly to one or another of the archetypal forms of music originating in different cultures: the emotional-tonal-rhythmic qualities inherent in Balinese, Slavonic, Latin-American, Scottish, Arabian, Oriental, and other ethnic music all have their therapeutic potential. The ability to improvise in all these styles is called for if the therapy is to attain its widest scope.

Each child's music becomes his, personally, and is almost always born out of the responses and events in the sessions. It is rarely possible to use one child's music for another, especially in the early stages of the therapy. As the children progress from session to session the music for each one will change and develop as he develops through his experiences. It will then come about that as a child frees and orders his responses and moves from one musical experience to another, he will progress naturally from the exceptional towards the universal.

Children work hard to extend their musical-emotional experiences. The exercise of their new-found abilities in partnership with the therapist gives them great personal satisfaction and the character of the sessions is often joyful and exuberant.

But the mood of the work with more severely handicapped children can be sombre and fraught with conflict. Not all can so directly approach experiences that incorporate form, mobility and expression, even when presented flexibly, as they can be in improvised music. Many live on the fringes of such experiential processes, are deeply unsure of them and reluctant to enter into them. Music therapy with these children often calls for an attitude best described as strong tenderness; the objective yet embracing warmth that can live in song and in the therapist's singing voice is important to them. Others who live in a deeper emotional twilight may begin their therapy with intense, rhythmically disorganized struggles on the drum as their unreached, undeveloped emotional forces first come to expression. Often the music to which they respond is highly dissonant, but it is always capable of development and change.

There are also children who live so remotely that it is hard to gain insight into their experiencing and interpreting of life. Theories of childhood deprivation resulting in emotional disturbance do not adequately explain the perceptible daily facts of their condition. These children are more than emotionally disturbed: they appear unable to find significance in any usual life context, incapable of assimilating any of the forms, modes, or expressions of normal life. Their profound estrangement excludes them from the ensouling experience of communicable human emotion. Their prevailing emotional condition evokes the image of an inhospitable landscape in which they are fated to live. One may live amid tempestuous storms, another in an icy wasteland; another may walk alone in a bleak, comfortless desert.

For such a child music can become something rare, evocative or consoling. It can become another landscape for him, one in which he will be able to find more than the limits of his own being. When therapy first begins his responses may be dull and his behaviour rejecting. But each time he comes to the therapy room the music reaches out to him, regardless of his state—accommodating him, seeking out his sensitivities, expressing his mood or filling his psychic emptiness with the colour and sounds of its harmonic-melodic life. It dispels his fear and invites his trust. A particular theme becomes important, he remembers it, comes to anticipate it. As his involvement increases, his face shows a mobility of awareness and feeling; the music builds in intensity, catching his mood and leading it onwards. There are sessions of anxious resistance as the hazards of discovery and increased activity arise, but in living through them the child and therapist come to know each other and the child's confidence in his music deepens. It becomes a secure, fertile landscape of experience in which he feels himself quickened into communicative response—a new emotional stream begins to flow, nourishing a new awareness of self and of expressive capability.

Within exceptional children live some of the deepest needs of humanity, needs that call for a clearer recognition. In some degree they live in all children but in the exceptional they are less obscured by the more superficial needs of everyday life. To understand and meet these needs we must widen our concepts of therapy—and hence our concepts of man. The approach to therapy is narrowed by thoughts that compare the exceptional to the normal; it is widened beyond measure by considerations that invest the individual in the universal. Universal humanity is far greater than any transitory norm. A therapy which has as a goal the freeing and development of the individual within universal human principles is more effective than one that aims merely to normalize. Universal values transcend the limited values of any one nationality or culture. Universal values can live in music. This is why music can become so important in the lives of exceptional children.

September 1961 — March 1962

Institute of Logopedics, Wichita, Kansas.
Residential and Out-Patient. Pathologies: aphasia in combination with retardation, cerebral palsy, blindness or loss of hearing. Ages: 22 months–16 years. Fourteen children received individual therapy; 210 sessions were given. Forty-four children took part in group activities.

Research in Individual Therapy

Instilling control of severe neuromuscular dysfunction through the motor expression of intense musical experience.

Relationship of speech rhythms to rhythmic patterns in music.

Personality integration on a high level of general function through the clinical organization and development of considerable inherent musical ability.

Rhythmic confusion in drum-beating as an expression of deep neuropsychiatric disorder.

Stimulation and mobilization of an inert, blind child through engaging musical sensitivity with special vocal and rhythmic techniques.

Use of repartee in the therapy situation to promote give-and-take and to liberate musical self-expression.

Overcoming ritualistic and bizarre behaviour patterns through fostering melodic responsiveness.

Development of vocal resourcefulness and confidence through creative singing.

Inducement of spontaneous yet controlled coordination of arms, previously lacking coordination due to CNS deficit, through drum and cymbal beating expressive of musical-emotional experience; this leading to a heightened positive awareness of self on an integrated physical-emotional basis.

Group Activities

Experimental musical activities with cerebral-palsied children ages 5 to 7.

hist-whist, *a setting of the poem by e. e. cummings for four musically-gifted aphasoid children.*

A Play: The Story of Artaban, *adapted from H. Van Dyke's* The Other Wise Man, *for a group of teen-age, variously handicapped boys and girls with speech problems. The dialogue of actors and speech chorus was functionally supported by music which intensified the dramatic content.*

Pif-Paf-Poltrie *used repeatedly with a specially selected group of younger children.*

IV

INDIVIDUAL MUSIC THERAPY: CATEGORIES OF RESPONSE

In the diversity of the work with individual children new practices and dimensions of musical interaction between child and therapist continued to emerge. The range of response now manifested in this and previous projects began to separate out into categories of activity and sensitivity, distinct yet interconnected. Each child's response could be seen to embody one or several categories of responsive behaviour. Therapeutic progress inducing changes of response—always entirely individual and essentially significant as communications of inner adventure—could then be registered as changes in, or displacements of, categories of response.

To formulate the therapy in these terms, categories of response were defined in co-authorship with Herbert Geuter. Martin Palmer, then directing the Institute of Logopedics, wrote the following introduction:

INTRODUCTION

THE PLACE OF music, throughout history, in the rehabilitative professions has only been vaguely assessed. Musical therapy as a speciality and an adjunct of psychiatry is relatively quite recent. For the last quarter of a century it has been noted that musical experiences have definite effects on the motor behaviour of cases of cerebral palsy and for me the study of the general effects of music in the aphasias of children and adults has been both fascinating and productive for many years.

The areas of brain subserving musical reception and

performance are practically invulnerable except in trauma from automobile accidents, etc., against which nature has not provided adequate safeguards. In addition, neuro-anatomico-physiological arrangements (which are beyond the scope of the study to describe) preserve musical integration in cases of maldevelopment, anomalies and lesions of the brain.

I agree with the authors that in the communicatively handicapped individuals there lies behind their silence a possibility of emergent development. Their musical approach is a way of reaching past the silence to the individual in order to bring him to potential fulfilment.

To put this to the test an experimental programme was carried out at the Institute of Logopedics by Dr Nordoff and Mr Robbins at my invitation through the fall and winter of 1961–62. Robert Ralstin of the staff of the Institute of Logopedics received training from Dr Nordoff and Mr Robbins in these methods and continued the project.

An extremely severe group of twenty-seven aphasoid children (of whom twenty-five completed the project) and eight cases of severely-involved cerebral palsied children were studied for measurement and improvement. The mean improvement in five possible factors was 2·7 with a standard deviation of ± 1·59. One case only showed no improvement; nine improved in every factor.

A paper: "Effects of A New Type of Music Therapy Upon Children With Neurological Disorders" by Martin F. Palmer, Paul Nordoff and Clive Robbins was read at the 1962 Convention of the American Speech and Hearing Association. This paper describes the project at the Institute of Logopedics in more detail.

The following article is the first publication to describe the work of a composer-pianist in this field. It is of unique interest, for this is the first time that a musician possessing highly-developed compositional skills has entered into an investigation of the musical responses of handicapped children.

In any exploration of the factors of music therapy the responses under observation will be determined by the aptness, pertinence, etc., of the music used. Hence, with a composer as therapist, we should expect the investigation to be more extensive and the responses more exactly analysed.

Music is improvised at the moment of clinical apposition to the patient. The response elicited—vocal, rhythmic or otherwise—is engaged at the instant it occurs and furthered by music modulated or developed according to its nature. In this way the intricate complex of musical response becomes subject to a mobile exploratory musical "sense".

The union of this musical "sense" with professional pianistic technique in the person of the therapist, enables the particular response of each handicapped individual to be set into a meaningful relationship with a special musical context. The response, so augmented, immediately becomes positively significant to the patient, while to the observer it becomes concretely established and clearly defined.

Much of the material contained in this article is entirely new and it seemed to the authors important that the results of their work should be published at this time. The attempt has been made, despite the limitations of the written word in describing the musical experience, to outline the elements of their methodology in order that the experiences gained may have the advantage of replication by others.

—Martin F. Palmer, Sc.D.

* * *

THE WORKING SITUATION

When a child enters the music room he finds a drum beside the piano. At the piano the therapist is seated. The child is encouraged to beat the drum, to "make music" with the therapist. The initial aims of the therapist will be to discover to what extent the child can make music, how he makes it, and what music-making means to him. The therapist will discover all this through the use of improvised music.

THE EXPLORATION

Through his initial exploratory improvisations which are suited to the child's beating and his behaviour, the therapist creates a situation that has potential both for diagnostic investigation and for therapy. The child responds both musically and personally. The quality and extent of these responses determine the course of the improvisation which is continually directed by the therapist to include the child within its compass of musical experience.

If a channel of musical communication exists between the therapist and the child and this channel is open and free, then they are in direct musical rapport. This musical companionship opens a way to unforeseen realms of experience.

If, however, a channel of musical communication has not yet developed, the therapist improvises music suitable to whatever responses the child can make. In the course of the session, the therapist, working with these responses, seeks to build a channel of communication. This process involves trial and error; each child's responses are unique.

A high-quality tape-recording is made of each session. The detailed study of this supplements and consolidates the impressions gained from the actual session. The child's response becomes subject to clearer definition and more exact description. All music or song material that has evoked a significant response is transcribed to manuscript for reference in subsequent sessions. It is used as the basis for developing the contact gained and ensures continuity of experience and activity.

The following list, Categories of Response, is based on observations of work done with 145 children. Of this number, 31 received between 3 and 10 sessions, while 40 have received extensive experiences of music therapy, once, twice, or thrice weekly for periods of time ranging from 6 weeks to 13 months. Sessions last in length from 10 to 30 minutes and average 15 minutes.

CATEGORIES OF RESPONSE

1. Complete Rhythmic Freedom.
2. Unstable Rhythmic Freedom.
   a. Psychological
   b. Neurological
3. Limited Rhythmic Freedom.
4. Compulsive Beating.
5. Disordered Beating.
   a. Impulsive
   b. Paralytic
   c. Compulsive-Confused
   d. Emotional-Confused
6. Evasive Beating.
7. Emotional-Force Beating.
8. Chaotic-Creative Beating.
9. Piano Playing.
10. Responses by Singing.
    a. Self-Expressive
    b. Corresponsive
    c. Tonal or Rhythmic Responses by Children without Speech
11. Responses to Singing.
12. Responses to Specific Musical Idioms.
13. Responses to Mood or Changes of Mood in Music.

1. *Complete Rhythmic Freedom*

Instantaneous sensitivity to all tempi, dynamics, rhythmic patterns and to the rhythmic structure of melodies; also the ability to beat them on the drum. Children who respond in this way usually show a measure of musical intelligence, i.e. not only an unhindered perception of music as sound, but a feeling for music as an expressive medium.

In this category of response, the child remains in self-control although actively responding to the stimulation of the music. There will be excitement, pleasure or other emotional responses. These, although subjective and personal, possess an objective quality; the child finds the natural expression of his personal experience in the immediate enhancement through drum and cymbal of the music from which his experience springs.

2. *Unstable Rhythmic Freedom*

Here there is rhythmic freedom and perception of music, but the response is marred or limited by the child losing self-control through an excessive reaction to the stimulus of the music. This can be of two kinds:

a. Psychological. Faced with the stimulating world of music and the possibilities the situation holds for self-assertive expression the child becomes disorganized in his activity. Within him there are needs or drives with which he identifies himself. These are expressed by over-dramatic drum and cymbal-beating and a tendency to prolong one particular mood. It can also be that he wants to lead the situation musically, but, since he is incapable of doing so, order, purpose and constructive possibilities are lost.

b. Neurological. The child cannot control himself in *accelerandi* and fast tempi, becomes over-excited and runs away in his beating: he is overwhelmed by his own physical activity and loses self-control. He may be caught in repeating rhythmic patterns once they are introduced and become so obsessed by beating these that he is heedless of the course of the improvisation. This defect is usually coupled with an insensitivity to musical dynamics. He may become fixed in beating different tempi once they are established in the improvisation. This may be accompanied by rocking and subsequent lapses of awareness of change in the music.

There is an emotional component within the child as he becomes caught up in such an obsessive response. But it appears that this is something that "happens" to him and not something that he does out of choice. The primary cause of this aberration appears to be organic. It differs from the *Psychological* response where the child feels that he himself chooses the way he acts.

3. *Limited Rhythmic Freedom*

This response is determined by a general lack of development. Both acuity of listening and facility of expression through the muscular system are impaired. The child may try, but there are long delays in his response and clumsiness in following tempi. His tempo range is often limited. He is usually unable to beat rhythmic patterns or melodic rhythms although sensitive to dynamics. He may possess the capacity to respond sensitively to tonal relationships but lacks feeling for tempi or rhythm.

4. *Compulsive Beating*

In this response the child beats inflexibly in one tempo or in a constricted range of tempo. His beating is unresponsive and continuous, and can carry a definite feeling of being compelled or impelled; or its quality may be perseverative, mechanical and lifeless. It can be without accents or variations in dynamics.

The child can appear to be aware of the music and its source, and even interested in it, but he is unable to relate his beating to it; the compulsive beat intervenes and prevents him uniting actively with the music, although he is disposed towards this. He may be totally engrossed in his compulsive beating, seeming to find a personal significance in it; he appears to be unaware of, or indifferent to the music. He can turn his compulsive beating from drum to cymbal and experience the stimulation the cymbal tone gives although remaining unresponsive to the improvisation. He may appear unaware of his beating and un-aware of the improvisation—this is rare.

5. *Disordered Beating*

a. Impulsive. The child responds positively to the improvisation although he has little or no capacity for directed rhythmic freedom, and is unable to sustain a beating effort. He beats impulsively, his use of the drum and cymbal (or piano keys) expressing the intensity of his experience. He may beat in short, impulsive, irregular patterns. His beating may begin with a surge of excitement and slow down as his impulse is exhausted.

b. Paralytic. The child is unable to beat in tempo or he may possess only a narrow range of rhythmic freedom due to lack of muscular coordination. Sometimes he is unable to coordinate one hand with the other and beats different tempi with each. This category differs from Category 4, *Compulsive Beating*, inasmuch as this child can participate in the music by beating with accented beats such as the first beat of a measure or the last beat of short melodic phrases. He is aware of the music and his struggle to realize his response is apparent.

c. Compulsive-Confused. When beating with two hands simul-taneously, the child's respective rates of beating are out of phase. He appears unaware of this confusion and also of the basic beat of the improvisation. He is insensitive to the conflict of these three tempi. His response is essentially distant and when at his most distant the disparity of phase is at its greatest. The more stimulated he is by particular musical experiences, the more synchronous his beating.

d. Emotional-Confused. The beating is out of phase but variably so, being a listless pattern of cross-rhythms when the child is passive and becoming more rapid, disturbed and violent as the child is stimulated.

6. *Evasive Beating*

The child avoids beating in time to the music. He may cease

to beat when the tempo of the improvisation is made to coincide with his, or may change the tempo himself to side-step collaboration. He may beat strongly to drown out the improvisation. This can be due to the child's fear of the experience—he is shocked by the sensation of the basic beat uniting with his own beating impulses. Or he may avoid participation because of an emotional inability to endure contact with the therapist.

7. *Emotional-Force Beating*

The drum is not used rhythmically or musically but only as a means of using strength and making noise. The child responds to the music and the drum by taking the opportunity for unchecked activity to bring into expression emotional and physical force. He is engrossed in fulfilling his emotional and muscular impulses in the amount of noise he can generate. There are no stable or constructive rhythmic responses. The cymbal can be used in the same way.

8. *Chaotic-Creative Beating*

This is an unformed beating that is hypercreative and insufficiently stable. It is related to the improvisation but subtly and unpredictably so. It may be impulsively playful. Although the child's beating appears to lack conscious direction he is not beating compulsively as in Category 4, for his beating is responsive to the music and not in a fixed tempo. Neither is it disordered as in Category 5, for, although it may be unregulated, it has a fragmentary and evanescent relationship to the music.

9. *Piano Playing*

The child taps rhythms or plays in the treble, bass or middle registers of the piano. Some children, particularly young ones, prefer to begin in this way. To put a young child at the drum is to set him apart from the therapist and perhaps demand from him too great a measure of independence. Bringing him to the piano avoids this and includes him in the therapist's activity; as the therapist is playing on the piano keys the child feels comfortably drawn to play with him.

Children often play tone-clusters with their whole hands. Such dissonances do not seem to disturb them—on the contrary, they appear to find them stimulating and pleasurable.

10. *Responses by Singing*

Some children—these have been mostly girls—respond by singing. For them the directly personal expression of using the voice freely in melodies, melodic tones and dynamics is immediately important.

a. Self-Expressive. A child can improvise a song in which the words and the specific melodic idiom express her feelings. Such singing out of an emotional need can even have the character of an aria.

b. Corresponsive. The child sings songs improvised or introduced by the therapist to suit particular situations in the therapy. Examples are: greeting songs, songs to accompany drum-beating, and good-bye songs. The singing of these gives the child particular personal pleasure.

c. Tonal or Rhythmic Responses by Children without Speech. Tonal, rhythmic, or exclamatory sounds are made by children with severe or total speech handicaps. This response frequently occurs to improvised music which the therapist finds to be emotionally significant for the child. The involvement in the experience activates the inherent urge for vocal expression; the music's melodic and/or rhythmic structure both evoke the form of the vocalization and support it.

11. *Responses to Singing*

The singing of a child's name or the improvising of special songs or other vocal material induces changes of behaviour. A child who is initially unable to be either rhythmically or vocally active can respond emotionally to the therapist's singing. Out of the character of the relationship this creates he can move or be led into outwardly active experiences.

12. *Responses to Specific Musical Idioms*

Competent instrumental and compositional skill on the part of the therapist can permit a wide variation of rhythmic complexity, vital tonal experience and harmonic creativeness. The therapist's impressions of the child, and the child's response to the situation guide the development of the kind of scale form, intervallic or chordal experience, quality of melodic expression, and degree of rhythmic complexity that is used. The therapist's intention is to develop the idiom the child can assimilate and which will engage him. *Idiom* therefore signifies the specific character of the improvisation. It may fall into any of the well-defined categories of music or it may be an original musical expression which belongs only to the particular needs of the child. The experience so mediated may be predominantly rhythmic, melodic, or structural. The idioms improvised in this way vary enormously from child to child. Music that is therapeutically effective for one child can be quite meaningless for another.

Children who cannot respond rhythmically or vocally almost always show a response to a clinically developed idiom. Changes in facial expression, posture, rhythmic body movements, and variations in breathing are observed.

13. *Responses to Mood or Changes of Mood in Music*

No music is devoid of emotional charge. The range of emotional experience that can be created in the therapy setting through improvised music is limitless. The mobility of improvisation, its selective development, and sensitive handling can invoke moods of varied quality, intensity and magnitude.

Children vary in their susceptibilities and responses to the deliberate modelling of mood through music. Some are strongly affected by it. These children are also usually sensitive to any changes of mood the improvisation brings about.

Synthesis of Response-Analysis

A review of the Categories of Response will show that responses numbered 2 to 8 represent difficulties or limitations in children perceived rhythmically in relation to the therapist's improvisations.

Category 9, *Piano Playing*, represents a modified therapy situation in which several of the preceding categories will be found.

Category 10, *Responses by Singing*, defines a different mode of response that can precede, accompany or follow any of the rhythmic categories.

Categories 11, *Responses to Singing*, 12, *Responses to Specific Musical Idioms* and 13, *Responses to Mood or to Changes of Mood in Music*, define responses of a personal or emotional nature that are specifically related to the creative activities of the therapist. For the sake of definition they are considered separately in this analysis from the rhythmic and vocal responses defined in Categories 1 to 10. However, it is obvious that in any working session they are not separate. Any response to the therapist's singing, to the musical idiom or to the resulting musical mood will be manifest in the child's beating or singing, where these expressive activities are possible. Therefore, where children can beat the drum or sing all responses are compound. The exceptions to this are to be found in Categories 4, *Compulsive Beating*, and 5, *Disordered Beating*, for here children can be unaware of the music. In all other categories they are aware of the music and so demonstrate responses within the range of Categories 11 to 13.

Working with the Responses

Categories 11 to 13 constitute the avenues for therapeutic

approach that children extend towards the therapist. Through them the therapist and child, by virtue of their inter-responsive activity in the living musical experience, can work together on such hindrances and malformations as are defined in Categories 2 to 10. The musical experience is the sphere of their activity; it is effected by the origination and modelling of idiom by the therapist and by the clinical techniques he uses to develop the child's response.

Examples

1. *A nine-year-old brain-damaged, aphasoid, autistic boy showing response Category 4, Compulsive Beating.*

What a compulsive beat signifies is an enigma. It is almost always associated with children generally described as autistic. Perhaps its most salient characteristic is its apparent meaninglessness; no variety, no mobility, no expression, remoteness. It is unrelated to the environment.

In this case there is, to begin with, no comprehension of the music on the part of the child. It appears that he finds significance only in the repeated action of beating: the repeated sensation of resistance from the drum-head and the percussive sound as the blow falls. This has nothing to do with music—as the inflexible rhythm and lack of accent verify.

Gradually the boy is attracted by two songs sung by the therapists; one is about him and contains his name (photo Appendix I, 7). His emotional response can initially come no further than facial expression and deeper breathing. His stiff posture relaxes to the warmth of the melodies and harmonies.

The songs alternate with rhythmic work, the therapist leading from one to the other as the child's responses indicate. Subjected to syncopation and dissonance in the improvisation his compulsive beat begins to break down. His beating now acquires some meaning and relates to the songs. Response 3,

Limited Rhythmic Freedom, gradually displaces the compulsive beating. Response 10c, *Tonal and Rhythmic Responses by Children without Speech*, develops as he begins to sing fragments of the songs with the therapist. As he works his way into musical expression through a series of new experiences, he activates parts of his nervous system he has not used before.

2. *A nine-year-old mongoloid boy shows responses* 8, *Chaotic-Creative Beating;* 9, *Piano Playing;* 12, *Responses to Specific Musical Idioms. (See also pages* 28 *and* 29.)

It is important that this child be musically stimulated—he himself must be allowed to improvise. The therapist does not try to impose musical order for this would inhibit the inherent creativeness of the child's ego. The responsive work of the therapist precipitates moments of musical perception which lead the child to relate his beating to the improvisation. At first, these fleeting responses consist of only one or two musically related beats, but they form the basis for therapeutic work which gradually secures the child's confidence in himself. He feels himself within the music and in beating can exteriorize his experience. He enjoys the musical give-and-take and anticipates the next working session (photos Appendix I, 4). His musical intelligence is realized gradually and the intimate rapport consolidates the work. Response 3, *Limited Rhythmic Freedom*, becomes established. A musical companionship arises which makes further therapeutic coactivity possible.

3. *A musically-gifted, aphasoid, emotionally disturbed seven-year-old girl shows the following responses:* 2a, *Unstable Rhythmic Freedom;* 7, *Emotional-Force Beating;* 10, *Responses by Singing a. Self-Expressive;* 11, *Responses to Singing;* 12, *Responses to Specific Musical Idioms;* 13, *Responses to Mood and Changes of Mood in Music.*

Her involuntary impulsiveness mars the musical experiences that are improvised. Dramatic music with unpredictable changes of mood engages her impulsiveness and calls forth a fountain of song. This free and unformed singing discloses a unique musical gift.

Musical discipline and constructive musical work on drum and cymbal clear up responses 2*a*. and 7. and establish response 1. In this process her innate gift for musical perception stabilizes her self-awareness.

A repeated, carefully-developed musical-dramatic experience deepens the child-therapist relationship and consolidates her inner life. These events enhance her singing: she finds meaningful words and sings them as an aria to express the tensions of her growing inner experience—this demands the use of specific musical idioms in the improvisation in order to set her moods to music. She masters speech handicaps as she explores the being of song (photos Appendix I, 5). This assumes a range of expression that in character is 10 to 12 years ahead of her age group. The attainment of this range of expression frees her from the internal confusion of emotional conflict from which she has suffered. She objectifies her inner life and discloses her personality to the therapists.

This begets a new appreciation of sensory experience as objects are invested in song. The dual process matures her personality. Later she becomes competent and sure in using her singing in group activities. She adopts a positive, active attitude to her environment.

This illustrates how the art of music as therapy can induce a sequence of personality changes which are consistent in building a solid and independent ego-organization. Music therapy has reached its goal and further developments go hand in hand with the attainment of skills and the assimilation of life experience.

CONCLUSION

The child displays its "musical geography" by answering to

improvisation. This the therapist orders and forms so that, as the work in the sessions expands, an incisive formative experience comes into being which is so closely related to the child's inmost self that a pure awareness of that self is aroused. New and exciting horizons of experience are lit up which are never forgotten and the child picks its flowers of experience in the meadows of its newly-acquired land. The measure of freedom achieved will allow it to engage in living in a new way and rebuild its previously disordered, disturbed or fragmented inner life.

V

EXPERIMENTAL GROUP ACTIVITY—
WORKING REPORTS

In the music therapy project at the Institute of Logopedics the mornings were devoted to individual therapy and the afternoons to group activities. We worked with four groups concurrently: The Pif-Paf-Poltrie group; a group of teenagers working on a play (see photo Appendix II, The Story of Artaban); a special group formed for advanced ensemble work (see photo Appendix II, hist-whist); and an experimental group containing severely disabled cerebral-palsied children. The purpose of this latter group was to see to what extent musical activation and social-musical interactivity might be developed with such children.

MIKE, LUCY, ALICE, MARVIN AND GENE comprised half the group. They wore football helmets to protect their heads, were fitted with a variety of braces and supported by special fixtures in sitting positions in their wheelchairs. Four other children, not so incapacitated, were included to facilitate the development of active musical experiences: Vera and Tom were cerebral-palsied but able to walk. Wendy was brain-injured and aphasoid, Ralph was mongoloid. All were between five and seven years of age.

In working with this group our impulse was to begin with a great deal of vitality, to sustain a continuous stream of creative musical experiences that would be stimulating and refreshing, which could give pleasure and invite participation.

October 3, 1961, Session 1.
Exploratory work to investigate the children's rhythmic and vocal possibilities, to get to know them, and to evolve some songs and activities as a basis for future work.

The entire session was improvised; we greeted the children musically and then worked with what they could do and with their reactions to what we did. We "danced" with them and sang about the dancing, clapped hands and sang about clapping. All the children's responses were kept alive. Wendy, contrary to expectation, was not at all shy. Mike put plenty of vigour into the activities and helped them along. Ralph was inhibited and stiff. Gene, though unable to do much, was very animated. Tom smiled and laughed but was reluctant to be brought into any activity; he wanted to stay on the periphery and observe it all from there, playing peek-a-boo from behind the door. After the dancing and hand-clapping we did some stepping around the room with Ralph. This was vigorous and woke him up somewhat. Mike wanted to do it. With the leader's support he marched vigorously around the room, jerking and stamping his braced legs vigorously. Then he played the piano, tapping the keys in the treble to an improvised song: "Mike is playing the piano." Wendy came to the piano. She "played" with care, using her hands gracefully, obviously imitating a pianist. It is difficult for her to play slowly. Then with Wendy playing in the bass, the pianist in the middle, and Mike in the treble, we played a "go-and-stop" game. On the shout of "go!" everyone began to play; on the shout "stop!" everyone stopped. We encouraged the children to play slow and fast in this game. This stimulated them and aroused their interest. They enjoyed it. Ralph did not use the same vigour as the other children but played feebly with one hand. We played the game again getting all the children to shout "stop!" and "go!" They were very good—Mike particularly so.

We wanted to get them singing. Melodies were improvised

to rhythmic speech phrases. As the children's names were sung
they began to join in. When the pianist sang Gene's name,
Mike, remembering that in the beginning of the session we had
sung about the children being "here", sang "is here!" Then
we sang a "tongue out" song, with the words, "Ralph is sticking
his tongue out." We sang the other children's names to the
song and they joined in this game with a great deal of pleasure.
Mike and Wendy sang. Tom wouldn't cooperate, so we sang a
song about "Tom is *not* sticking his tongue out." The other
children saw the joke and sang it with us.

We got out the drum and asked the children what it was. No
one said that it was a drum, so we suggested that it was all kinds
of improbable things. Some of these were very funny and a
"laughing song" was improvised. The children liked this and
we all laughed as we sang it. Ralph was the first to beat the
drum. To begin with he was stiff and unable to respond very
freely; he became "stuck" in tempi. But gradually he improved
and became more alive. He enjoyed using the cymbal, and
became more vigorous. His face unfroze for a moment or two.
Wendy came to the drum and beat firmly from the beginning.
It is difficult for her to beat a slow tempo, but she accelerates
beautifully. Mike beat so loudly and quickly that he couldn't
hear the music. We taught him to beat more slowly and quietly;
he soon became able to beat fast and slow. He sang and shouted
as he beat but many times picked up the tempo of the music.
To control him a bit, the "go-and-stop" game was reintro-
duced. He joined in this with enthusiasm.

The drum was taken to Gene. His arm was extremely stiff
and he had great difficulty in bringing the stick down to the
drum, but he tried hard and, although it was difficult to judge,
we felt that the experience was rewarding for him. A song was
improvised about the children and what they were doing. Mike
freely joined in singing it. When the pianist sang to a quasi-
Spanish style of music, Mike sang with exuberance and freedom, reaching some very high notes. When Tom's turn came

his beating was heavy and violent; there was no give-and-take. While the pianist was working with Tom, Wendy jumped up, went to the piano, and began to play it with him. We finished the session with the *Good-bye* song. The pianist played the melody with Wendy's finger. The children's names were included in the song.

October 17, 1961, Session 3.
Various musical instruments used to explore the possibilities of developing a story with songs and instrumental parts. Blowing instruments reveal muscular difficulties and limitations in breath control. Some gains in rhythmic freedom evident.

We began the session in the usual way, singing to the children and improvising songs about their activities. This time there was also a song about the clothes they were wearing. Then various blowing instruments were tried to see if it would be any easier for the children to blow than to beat the drum and cymbal. We began with a small horn. Many of the children had difficulty in closing their mouths around it and some had difficulty in blowing at all.

Mike and Ralph were the only children who could blow the horn. Ralph immediately began a give-and-take with the improvisation, imitating a rhythmic pattern exactly in the tempo. We tried a bamboo flute, hoping this would be easier for the other children as it could be placed against a closed mouth and blown with the lips opened a little. Mike blew it, but felt that he had to sing the note himself at the same time. He could blow single notes, but could not imitate the simple rhythmic pattern of two quavers followed by a crotchet rest. All the children watched with great interest.

Vera took the flute in her hand and really worked hard to put it to her mouth and blow. It was difficult for her to do this, but she succeeded and blew it many times. We sang a "Good Girl!" song. As Alice, Gene, Lucy, Tom, and Wendy had not succeeded in making a note, a very small flute was taken to each child and put to one nostril while the other was held closed. All were able to produce a note in this way and were very pleased to do it. Some children could even blow louder and softer.

Then the slide-whistle was demonstrated and the children were delighted with it. We tried to get Mike to move the slide up and down as he blew. This required arm movements as well as breath control, and he could not do it. Ralph did very well. When it was Wendy's turn she succeeded in blowing two or three short notes. She was standing by Gene, who, with a very clear purpose in mind, reached over from his wheel-chair with a tremendous effort, grasped the end of the slide and began to move it. We asked Ralph to blow it for Gene. Gene moved the slide up and down with great pleasure and together they produced many notes. The children were intrigued and all wanted to take turns. The leader blew it for Alice. As she was moving the slide, he blew short repeated notes instead of a sustained note. This made the whistle produce a sort of laughing sound. The pianist improvised a "Laughing Bird" song, which was much like the laughing song used in previous sessions. The children really enjoyed this and Alice got great pleasure from being the instrumentalist in this song. Then the whistle was taken around and all the children made the "laughing bird" laugh. Mike wanted to try again—by himself. He took a mighty breath and succeeded in blowing fortissimo and sliding at the same time.

The children took turns on the drum. Wendy beat rather quietly. Her beating was a little unsteady. Twice she responded to the quavers in the melody, but in the uncertain efforts she made to beat them she lost the basic beat. To stimulating music she beat just a little faster, but harder and steadier. To the waltz, "Beautiful Wendy", she beat a fixed tempo that was between 110 and 120 beats per minute—she has beaten this tempo on many occasions. In a Spanish improvisation that followed, she made a fine *accelerando* up to 160 and 170 bpm.

As the music went on accelerating Wendy became confused, but finally her beating steadied and she could be accompanied at 210 bpm. We tried to get her to imitate the rhythm of her name. The leader beat it once to show her. She "got it" and alternated this rhythm with the piano twice before she lost the ability to do it.

Tom beat in time to a heavily-accented waltz and used the cymbal intelligently and musically to mark the ends of phrases. As the pianist worked with him, Ralph blew the horn. This led to an improvisation in the key of the horn note; Tom beat, and Ralph showed his sensitivity to the cadence by blowing his horn on the final chord. Vera beat with a great deal of strength but in a fixed tempo between 100 and 120 bpm. She was serious and attentive. Mike's beating was much more controlled. He gets different tempi more quickly now and at one time we could encourage him to beat with a big swing of his arm. All the time the children were beating, the pianist continued to work with Ralph who was still blowing the horn. He learned to hold a long note and then to blow the horn at definite times in a short improvisation, repeatedly playing, in a rest, a duplet that completed a musical phrase. This led to a horn and piano give-and-take. He played with precision.

Alice's beating was unsteady, but she beat for a longer time than last week. Gene, too, showed more facility in his beating although he hasn't yet sufficient control to get a musical experience from it. He wanted to play the big cymbal and did so with great determination. Lucy also played the big cymbal and then, with a small stick, beat on the tambourine which the leader held in a favourable position for her cramped and jerky arm movements. She did much better than in the last session.

We sang the *Good-bye* song and as the children were leaving, the pianist repeated it, playing the melody with Vera's finger. Her arm was so stiff it was impossible for her to move it accurately in the rhythm of the song.

* * *

In the fourth session a new child was added to the group. Faith was an eight-year-old, musically-gifted girl with a beautiful voice who had emerged from severe emotional disturbance in four months of individual therapy. (See pages 72 and 73, photos Appendix I, 5 and also photo Appendix II, *hist-whist*.) In this particular group activity she could extend her development further. For her to help more handicapped children in an active musical setting would give her a special form of social experience in which she could find a way to use her musical gifts objectively. We felt Faith needed to do this. We also hoped that her inherent musical vitality would bring joy and pleasure to the other children.

She adopted the role of a "teacher", modelled her behaviour on ours, and to the full extent of her abilities gave us loyal help.

November 7, 1961, Session 6.
Social-music therapy for Faith—she finds her musical orientation in the group. Most children show marked improvement in rhythmic facility. A wider variety of instruments in use. Breath control and handling improve in playing blowing instruments. A theme for a story emerges.

Faith arrived a few minutes before the other children. As she is very eager to be tall and is convinced that she is growing every day, we have to measure her each time she comes into the music room. Today we measured her against the piano and piled a drum and a few small boxes on it until we reached the right height. She is learning to whistle and whistled to an improvisation. She did not whistle a melody, but held notes which she changed to suit the harmony. In response to her eager demand that we notice how long her hair was growing (another daily request), the pianist improvised a calypso song: "Faith's Hair Is Growing Longer Every Day." During this song the other children began to arrive. Faith played the piano with the pianist and Mike was given a drumstick to beat the drum. We sang the words "every day" repeatedly, singing them antiphonally with the melodic-rhythmic pattern played on the piano. Mike beat both the basic beat and the rhythmic pattern and sang along with us. The song continued while all the children entered. As they came in they were given flutes, whistles, and horns. That is how today's work came to begin with a jam session on "Faith's Hair Is Getting Longer Every Day". The song ended with whoops of laughter. We evicted the helpers who had brought the children and who had been unable to tear themselves away, and in the exuberant, happy mood created by the song, greeted the children.

Wendy's song "Beautiful Wendy Is Here with Me", was used as a greeting song; in turn the other children's names were put to it. Alice was wheeled to the drum and tried painstakingly to beat the melodic rhythm of "Beautiful Alice Is Here with Me". She succeeded when the song was played slowly. Her beating improved and she deliberately hit the cymbal at the end of the song. Gene was next. His beating is getting better every week, though he is not yet able to beat a basic beat. We tried to put some form into his beating by getting him to beat the drum and cymbal alternately. Then it was Lucy's turn; she beat stronger than ever before. The pianist wanted her to become aware of and beat a simple melodic rhythm. He played the rhythm of two quavers and a crotchet. When this had been repeated four or five times Faith suddenly sang out very rhythmically, "Uncle Paul!"* She sang it in the rhythm and tempo of the rhythmic pattern. She had understood what the pianist was attempting and sang "Uncle Paul" repeatedly in her efforts to help Lucy beat this pattern. We played a little game of rhythmic patterns after this. Lucy beat a great deal, and began to hit the cymbal fairly regularly. She was getting very near to beating the basic beat and was pleased with herself.

Faith helped to adjust the height of the drum for Ralph.

* Young children call the authors "Uncle Paul" and "Clive".

Rhythmic patterns were tried with him but he wanted to beat a basic beat. He was very responsive and beat vigorously for a long stretch in different tempi. Ralph is waking up and losing his timidity! Wendy surprised us by beating the basic beat of "Beautiful Wendy Is Here with Me" quite perfectly. When we came to the final cadence, the pianist held the last note back, waiting for her to beat the cymbal. Mike, who watches everything intently, just had to sing it to fill the pause. After this Wendy beat a good basic beat to a faster improvisation. When triplets were played against a duplet rhythm in the improvisations she tried to beat the triplets and succeeded for a moment or two.

Faith needed to sing her own song, the song that had been so important in her individual therapy: "Faith Is Dancing a Song." She was tense when she began and sang it quietly. As she gained confidence she sang it romantically and then passionately. Finally at our request she sang it carefully for the children. When she sang the words, "dreaming, dreaming", Mike, gazing up at her in rapture through his thick-lensed glasses, had to sing them softly with her. As the song finished he burst into spontaneous applause in which all the children joined.

When Mike was asked to beat the drum he insisted on having two sticks. Ralph had been given the horn. We began an improvisation which led into Faith's song, and she sang it with full voice. Mike was beating the basic beat and Ralph was blowing the melodic rhythm. Suddenly, for a few bars, it became an operatic duet between Faith and the pianist. Lucy began to beat the cymbal; several children joined in the singing. While we were all playing or singing someone blew the slide-whistle. The laughter this aroused broke up the improvisation. We laughed a "laughing song", which led directly into the "Laughing Bird" song. We worked with this. Between the repetitions, as the slide-whistle was taken from one child to another, Faith was moved many times to sing her own song.

But she was able to stop each time we recommenced the "Laughing Bird" and sing it with us. She is becoming an asset in the class; her singing is a glorious addition.

Gene learned to blow a flute today! Wendy learned to blow the "miaow" on the cat-call in "The Cat Wants Her Milk"! While we were working on this, Gene on the other side of the room and undirected, blew his flute—for the first time—at the *right* moment in the song. Then we improvised a little story. Gene blew his flute for a mouse. Mike played the slide-whistle for the laughing bird. Wendy played the cat-call. There was a thunder-storm in which Faith made drum-rolls. Lucy hit the cymbal for lightning. Faith made rain with her fingers on the drum. Ralph blew his horn for a cow that wanted to be milked. When asked, he blew it very gently and quietly. Then Lucy wanted to try a flute. Gene passed her his. She succeeded! Immediately Gene leaned over and, with that great effort, took his flute straight back. Alice was not able to succeed today. We spent some time teaching Wendy to blow the cat-call at the right time in the song, and to sing the words, "the cat wants her milk, oh, the cat wants her milk". She finally blew the "miaow" at more or less the right time and sang the words carefully but so quietly as to be barely audible. Following the *Good-bye* song, while the children were having their coats put on, Faith danced with Wendy to *Beautiful Shoes*. The *Good-bye* song was repeated with Ralph's finger.

* * *

At this point we left the story of the cat, the mouse, the bird, etc., in order to develop a Christmas theme.

November 14, 1961, Session 7.
Blackboard picture-making, story-telling and piano improvisation are combined to illustrate the content of a Christmas carol. The cast for a Christmas scene begins to form.

After greeting the children, we began to work on a Christmas story with them. We used an old English carol, *The Friendly Animals*.* It has a beautiful directness and simplicity, perfect for children of this age.

> *"I," said the Donkey all shaggy and brown,*
> *"I carried His mother to Bethlehem town,*
> *I carried His mother to Bethlehem town,*
> *I," said the Donkey all shaggy and brown.*

> *"I," said the Cow all white and red,*
> *"I gave Him my hay to pillow His head,"* etc.

> *"I," said the Sheep with the curly horn,*
> *"I gave Him my wool to keep Him warm,"* etc.

> *"I," said the Dove on the rafters high,*
> *"I sang Him to sleep so He would not cry,"* etc.

We turned the children's chairs so that they could face the blackboard and the leader described the scene set in the carol by telling the nativity story, drawing pictures on the blackboard as he did so. The pianist accompanied this with improvised music, leading it into the melody of the carol whenever appropriate to the story. The children were enthralled as they watched a picture appear in which, amid falling snow, Joseph led a donkey carrying Mary. Gradually the picture disclosed that they were approaching a stable in which were the cow, the sheep, and the dove. The Angel appeared, carrying the infant Jesus. The children were utterly attentive. As the story told of the animals' parts in the nativity scene, we sang the verses of the carol. The pianist would sing a verse through once and we would all join in as best we could and repeat it. The children

* Nordoff and Robbins, *The Second Book of Children's Play-Songs* and *The Children's Christmas Play*.

came or were wheeled to the blackboard and pointed to each animal as it was named. When Vera was asked what part she would like to play, without any hesitation she pointed to the drawing of Mary.

We began to make the carol into a tableau. Tom took the part of Joseph. Seated on the donkey's back (the leader's) Vera was led solemnly by Tom to the stable. Here Ralph played the cow, Wendy the sheep, and Marvin the dove. Faith, who we hoped would sing the carol, played the part of the Angel. After this first "rehearsal" of the tableau, we wanted to see what parts the other children could possibly play in the story. Alice, Lucy, Gene and Mike were put on the floor to see whether they could crawl. Mike and Lucy did well, well enough to take a part. Alice and Gene were quite helpless. While we were all gathered around the manger, Faith went to the piano and began to learn the four verses of the carol. The pianist found himself improvising a fifth verse about the Angel.

The improvising of music to accompany and express each part of the story gave a unity of mood to the picture-making, the story-telling, and the acting. It was a warm, intimate mood in which the children were relaxed and completely absorbed in everything that happened. It stayed with us in the four sessions that followed, giving us all a deeper experience of Christmas.

VI

PIF-PAF-POLTRIE, THE WORKING GAME AS THERAPY

We were given the freedom to choose children to make a special group for Pif-Paf-Poltrie *and to repeat the game with them once weekly over a two-month period. In doing this we learned that there was much more in this game than we had realized when it was first developed—even though our early experiences of the children's responses to it had impressed us. We began to use it with a more clinical attitude, becoming increasingly aware of its cumulative effects. As a working-game,* Pif-Paf-Poltrie *came to be an entirely new form of group therapy. It combined several aspects of music therapy with speech exercise, ring-game activities, and a kind of drama therapy which centred on a formative, universal experience—all having simplicity and directness.*

The idea of the game; the dialogue and form of its "story".

The origination of the game of *Pif-Paf-Poltrie* at Sunfield occurred in the spring of 1959 during a study being made by the staff of a severely handicapped and isolated boy. Herbert Geuter, who was leading the study, suggested to Robbins, then the child's class teacher, that a possible means of creating an effective contact could lie in a game made out of the tale of *Pif-Paf-Poltrie*. "Not a story," he said, "but a game."

It is a little known folk-tale,* in fact hardly a tale at all, consisting of less than a page of dialogue in question and answer

* "Fair Katrinelje and Pif-Paf-Poltrie", *Grimm's Fairy Tales*, (London: Routledge and Kegan Paul, 1948), p. 593.

form. The gist of it is that Pif-Paf-Poltrie wants to marry Fair Katie. He must ask her father, sowing wheat, her mother, milking the cow, her brother, chopping wood, and her sister, cutting cabbages, each in turn, for their permission. His meetings with them are in the nature of a ritual; as each gives consent, he or she makes the condition that the others must also agree, and names them in sequence. Having gained everyone's approval, Pif-Paf-Poltrie asks Fair Katie herself. She accepts—in the same form of dialogue—and tells him what she has for a dowry when they are married. She goes on to ask him what he can do: is he a tailor? a cobbler? a farmer? To each question he answers, "Better than that!" Is he a joiner? a blacksmith? or a miller? He answers as before. Finally she calls out, "You're a besom-binder!" To this Pif-Paf-Poltrie says, "Yes! Isn't that a fine job!"

This is how the tale ends. There is no prince, no enchanted princess, no giant—just a down-to-earth dialogue between a group of people all busy working.

The practical and musical development of the game.

At the beginning of the autumn term Robbins began to develop a form for the action of the game with his children. One day they went out into the grounds; together they cut down a young birch, made a besom, and swept some of the early fallen leaves. The children enjoyed this and it seemed then that a realization of the game would have to include the making of a besom with which Pif-Paf-Poltrie could sweep up leaves. It was at this time that Nordoff arrived and was asked to compose music for the game. Collaborative work with and around the children's animated responses led to the integration of speech, songs, action and music in a unified form.

The completed game began with the making of the mess of leaves on the floor of the classroom; the besom was then taken apart and its twigs scattered over the leaves. Three children took the parts of Pif-Paf-Poltrie, Father Hollyberry, and Fair Katie, and after introductory music and speech, the action began. A spirited march accompanied Pif-Paf from meeting to meeting with the members of the family as they entered the game. With a simple lyric song Fair Katie described her dowry to him. The mood of the game quickened with a working song which all the children sang, asking Pif what kind of work he did while they made the actions of each trade in the song's rhythm. Then singing "You're a Besom-Binder!" they gathered the birch twigs. To verses of the besom-binding song, Pif-Paf and the teacher put the besom together and bound it. This led to the game's climax, the sweeping of the leaves into a tidy heap by Pif-Paf. As he worked he was supported by music and an encouraging sweeping song. The game finished with rhythmically spoken questions, shouted answers, and joyful singing. The leaves were replaced in a basket to an "and they all lived happily ever after" song.

The responses of the children. Games: their purposes and contents.

The game was frequently used with groups of ten to twenty children and occasionally with groups of up to fifty. It always met with an aroused, attentive response. The children were eager to repeat it. The role of Pif-Paf-Poltrie was sought by almost every boy; many made unexpectedly strong efforts to accomplish the part and the groups, composed of very varied children, gave them good support. The game took from thirty to forty-five minutes, depending on the age and development of the children in the group.

It became increasingly clear why Dr Geuter had suggested a game, rather than a story. The game realized the action of the tale *practically*; the children could invest their attention and effort in its formed activities. Its meaning became concretely comprehensible to them; they could carry its purpose as a personal impulse or ideal.

All group games are forms of social integration; many aim in their structure for the attainment of a mutual goal through individual skill and initiative—hence their importance as mediators of both individual development and social inter-action. There are relatively few games that mentally or emotion-ally handicapped children can play with pleasure and success. They are either unable to grasp the purposes of most games, or are not stable or quick enough to play them properly. Their play-ing is so often solitary or bizarre. When they play together their games frequently become aimless and their playing peters out.

The clarity of the goal of Pif-Paf-Poltrie as a game made it attractive to the children at Sunfield; the central action of sweeping up the mess aroused their interest and, when suc-cessfully completed, yielded a sense of satisfaction. The form of the game could focus their concentration. The use of music served to characterize and enliven each part of the action for them, the different qualities of the songs modelling their experiences throughout its structure. Most pervasive was their enjoyment of the *good feeling* of the game; the sweeping up of the mess assumed for them an expression of moral purposeful-ness. We saw this same mood of involvement wherever the game was subsequently enacted. On the European tour one psychologist, prompted by the children's absorption as Pif swept, remarked, "There is a benediction on that sweeping!"

The game was used with two groups at the Devereux Schools for a few sessions and responses were observed that were directly reminiscent of those at Sunfield and on the tour. It was also used intermittently with psychotic-autistic children at the University of Pennsylvania's Day-Care Unit. Here some sur-prisingly overt responses occurred while many others of significance were evoked.

The selected group for the game. The progression of involvement.

The Pif-Paf-Poltrie group at the Institute of Logopedics was specially constituted. As its nucleus, six children were chosen for whom behavioural control would be no problem. They were at the age and stage of development to enjoy the game, its action and its songs. With them were included an equal number of children who were usually less responsive, but who we felt could be drawn into activity with the stimulation and support of the others. About half of the children were resident at the institute; the rest came in daily for treatment and special education. Some had brain-injury of unknown ætiology, others were cerebral-palsied but able to walk unaided; there were aphasoid and mongoloid children. All presented various degrees of retardation and a variety of speech difficulties. In temperament and age they ranged from a delicate, blonde, intensely trusting, observant five-year-old girl, to a robust, but quiet, shy eight-year-old mongoloid boy; from a six-year-old, determined, dark-eyed, cerebral-palsied girl with poverty in her background, to a plump, nervous, brain-damaged girl who found her security in "adopting" a younger boy.

With this group we found that the experience the game created was one which could grow continually for almost every child. It became apparent that because its general activities of singing, rhythmical movement and speech were united in a structure, they offered not only a means for group coactivity but also opportunities for individual developmental involvement. These could lead a child from peripheral participation, step by step to the carrying of the central role of Pif-Paf-Poltrie and so to sustaining the entire sequence and purpose of the game. Once the action was set and maintained by the children who spontaneously appreciated and took up the game, those who were not at first so freely able to join in found points of contact through which they would begin to relate themselves to its structure. There were many such openings for initial participation—the singing of words or phrases of songs, the making of movements in the working song, the picking up of birch twigs, the shouting of "Yes!" to the questions, the replacing of leaves in the basket—and children individually took the one that most stimulated or invited them. From an initial response of this kind a child's activity in the game would progressively expand in further sessions until it became possible for him to take one of the secondary character parts. When this stage was attained, the way was usually open to the role of Pif. In their progress children were warmly supported, but were left as free as possible to realize their own volition and abilities.

The children's individual speech difficulties were manifested in the dialogue between the characters. We worked with these difficulties in the on-going context of the game, encouraging the children and aiming at progress through exposure to the game's repetitions and to other children's efforts, and through the influence of the leader's speech. We sought for the best a child could do *out of his involvement*; a demanding approach was avoided.

As the children came to know the game they became increasingly earnest in enacting the parts and in watching the progress of the action. A particular mood was engendered which deepened as the sessions were repeated to become a mood of group concentration embracing all the children in the important moments of the game. In this mood, those naturally disposed or able to recognize purposefulness in the efforts of others, expressed immediate personal concern; less integrated children, for whom any experience of positive commitment was initially weak or confused, were drawn steadily into increasing attentiveness.

The establishment of individual commitment. Participation overcomes pathological effects.

All responses and response developments were individual; each child started from where he was and made his own way into the experience.

Peter . . . (*mongoloid*): Very enthusiastic all along. Quite a lot of speech; utterly attentive the whole time; joined in the actions with pep. When he was Pif a revealing thing happened: after the besom was made and he was left alone to sweep, he looked at the mess and gave up. Negative experience had robbed him of confidence. He gave the leader the besom and sat down. He was given it back and with quiet encouragement he began to sweep. It took him over twelve minutes, working with care and growing pleasure, to sweep up the mess.

Dennis . . . (*cerebral palsy*): Open and enthusiastic from the beginning. Nicely appreciative of humour; plenty of good will. Despite his hindrances in movement, he swept most carefully and thoughtfully, and was quietly proud when he had finished. He learned all the words of the game very quickly and spontaneously spoke Pif's lines at the right time without prompting.

Mary . . . (*brain-injured*): Always worked hard; was a great help in singing the songs. She was surprised at the amount of work required in being Pif when it was her turn, but she faced up to it.

Carl . . . (*mongoloid*): Was the very first Pif and did it well. He wanted to be Pif nearly every time. At first not attentive to the others, but this improved steadily; always happy to be in the sessions. He spoke well and was consistently dependable in any part he took.

Felice . . . (*brain-injured, aphasoid*): She was full of wonder towards everything that happened. Her response to the speaking part was very good. Although usually she only spoke in single words, in the game she tried to say every line complete. She worked hard at articulation using, for her, considerable volume. She began to sing, and "sang" more freely each session. She had a high voice that wandered sweetly over a wide range of notes. She was not yet able to sing a definite melody. A game girl; did a very good job of sweeping when she was Pif.

Rose . . . (*cerebral palsy*): Together with Felice, Rose had known us since the project had begun in the previous September; she had grown to be warmly responsive to the content and goals of music therapy. In the sessions she became more of a colleague than a student. Always utterly concerned with the game in progress, she made a valiant Pif-Paf herself. Inevitably she had great difficulty in handling the besom—not so much in aiming and starting a sweeping stroke as in finishing the movement and controlling the spring of the twigs. Many times she swept the leaves too hard into the heap and scattered it. Undaunted, she put the heap straight each time this happened. One could see by her face that she regretted this recurring accident, but she showed no sign of distress or of giving up. We had too much respect for the determination that was living within her to offer any more than the most peripheral help. She was deeply happy and satisfied when she had finished and was pleased by our pride in her.

Julianna . . . (emotionally disturbed, aphasoid): Was admitted experimentally to the group for the early sessions, but the situation proved to be unsuitable for her. The other children were having their experiences disrupted by her behaviour and she was not getting enough from the game at this time to warrant the disturbance she made. She was withdrawn from the group and five more children were admitted.

Cora . . . (emotionally disturbed, aphasoid): Through illness, or timetable confusion, she came only twice. The first time she was evasive, teasing the student-assistant. The second time she was more attentive. She showed a grasp of the structure of the game and was intrigued by the binding of the besom—she got up from her chair several times to take a closer look. She also joined freely in the larger actions of the working song.

Angie . . . (brain-injured, spastic): Very friendly and open. Remembered us and *Pif* from the demonstration last June. Keen to take part, she always spoke well and made a very good Pif herself. She had a most possessive relationship to Ben though this was not always to Ben's taste.

Ben . . . (brain-injured, aphasoid): Timid and quiet to begin with (Angie's baby), but freed himself more and more from Angie and surprised us in the very last session by firmly requesting to be Pif. He did extremely well. He worked hard. He most definitely *wanted* to undertake the *whole* experience of being Pif. Twice in the speaking parts, his capacity for sustained attention lapsed and his speech became jumbled and meaningless. Of his own will, he took charge of his straying consciousness and brought it back to the situation. The same thing happened in the sweeping. The mess was extensive, and at times he lost his orientation within it; either he would sweep in a meaningless direction or he would sweep over the same place many times, his face becoming blank. Then he would pull himself together again, and sizing up the situation, sweep once more with purpose and intelligence. He went after out-lying leaves and swept them to the centre with careful control. Towards the end of his sweeping the leader helped him by gathering the isolated leaves into small heaps. He then swept these into the centre. It was deeply thrilling to see Ben become as active and integrated as this, to see him take charge of the situation, and work at it, *working on himself* as he did so.

Pif-Paf-Poltrie's sense of responsibility: his fulfilment. The inter-action of group commitment and individual effort.

When the child playing Pif-Paf sweeps, the others watch. Perhaps at first this watching is a mere interest in the new action, in the novelty of it, but the interest deepens as the game is repeated. Those who have "done a Pif" themselves feel a certain identity with the sweeper and an active concern over the task. Those yet to do it see still another of their companions undertaking this responsible activity. The business of "sweeping up that mess" becomes everyone's concern. The wish to see it done properly and completely grows in each child. This comes to be characteristic of the game.

The child who sweeps does so with everyone's attention upon him. At first, some children may be disposed to enjoy this too superficially—others might find it unbearable. It is the de-votion to the sweeping and all it comes to mean in the context that overrides such personal hindrances. Through his devotion the sweeper experiences the game's reality and achieves its essential fulfilment. The benefits of the more outward and social rewards follow the accomplishment of Pif's part naturally and in a balanced way.

The children share deeply in each other's efforts in the game. More or less consciously, they know the usual characteristics or limits of each other's behaviour. When they see a friend become active in the situation that they have all helped to create and in which they all share, as they watch him become purposeful and perhaps work hard to overcome a physical or behavioural impairment, they experience a deepening of interpersonal relationships on a positive, generative moral level. They develop a feeling of loyalty towards the task of Pif-Paf, and recognize each other's efforts to accomplish it. In this way everyone's attempts become therapeutic for the whole group.

That Rose did not give up when she oversWept the heap was due in some measure to the care of Mary and the striving devotion of Felice when they had swept. Having watched them, Rose could bring a determination to the situation that enabled her to overcome her besetting difficulties. Rose's perseverance in turn inspired Ben and gave him both the intention and the will to sustain the control of his own capacities. *This* is the Pif-Paf-Poltrie experience.

Several times in repetitions of the game, we have seen a child who is usually insecure and who chatters a good deal, fall silent during the sweeping and watch every sweep that Pif-Paf makes. Eventually, that child too has asked to be Pif-Paf. This happened to Caroline, and in that last session, she raised her hand to be Pif. Now it is up to the therapist, or teacher, to decide whether a child's desire to be Pif is backed by a resolve strong enough to face the challenge of the actual situation. It was decided that Caroline was not yet quite ready for her Pif and so Ben, who had asked so firmly, was chosen. It would not hurt Caroline to wait. It would be less damaging for her than a failure to carry the role. When her turn does come, and she is ready for it, she will take a sure, successful step on to a new plane of self and social experience.

May 1962—May 1967

MUSIC THERAPY PROJECT FOR PSYCHOTIC CHILDREN UNDER 7
(N.I.M.H. Grant number OM-982.)

The Day-Care Unit, Department of Child Psychiatry, School of Medicine, University of Pennsylvania.

The project that was conducted at this Unit from February–July 1961 (page 48ff.), tested the applicability to childhood autism of approaches and techniques previously developed with brain-injured, mentally and/or emotionally handicapped children. The effectiveness of this pilot demonstration led Mitchell Dratman, M.D., and Bertram A. Ruttenberg, M.D., directors of the Day-Care Unit, to apply to the National Institute of Mental Health for a grant to support a comprehensive three-year project. This was planned to include treatment, research, training and publication. The application was approved and N.I.M.H. Grant Number OM-982 awarded—to the authors' knowledge, the first federal grant entirely for music therapy research. In 1965 a supplementary grant from the N.I.M.H. extended the project for a further two years.

Twenty-six children received regular music therapy sessions. Their predominant age-range was from 4 to 6 years. At least 15 children were in an extreme autistic state; others were severely ego-disturbed with autistic features. Symbiotic behaviour was also much in evidence and there was one classically schizophrenic child.

Some mild to moderate organic involvement was suspected in 7 or 8 children and to some extent verified by long-term differential diagnosis.

Approximately 1,100 sessions were given, all tape-recorded, with the assistance of trainee therapists.

Research in Individual Therapy.

The study of the manifold influences of a long-term music therapy programme upon the development of autistic children.

This development was special to the circumstances of the Unit and the music therapy procedures, and varied with each child. Its starting point in each case was determined by the child's condition, and its course, in terms of both general and musical behaviour, showed itself as progress or movement within three critical areas of psychological assessment: (1) Relationship, (2) Communicativeness, (3) Musical comprehension and mastery.

The sensitivity of young autistic children and the difficulties involved in their treatment furthered the evolution of delicate, searching techniques in the improvisations used. These became effective in eliciting responses and/or changing behaviour. Through improvisations the children's responses were carefully fostered so that their activities could expand naturally as their involvement increased.

Vocal responses became of primary importance especially with children who had no speech. In several cases crying or screaming became crying-singing (tonally related to the music), which then became singing. Some children initiated new speech sounds, words or phrases during the course of therapy.

The defences of childhood autism could be penetrated by music therapy of this kind. The psychological development that ensued with many of the children treated was often a subtle blending of maturational growth and progress in the Day-Care Unit with specific gains resulting from the build-up of special experiences and activities in music therapy.

Group Activities

Pif-Paf-Poltrie *was used for intermittent periods; special groups of 2, 3, or 4 children were formed for structured or free instrumental activities.*

VII

MUSIC THERAPY AND PERSONALITY CHANGE IN AUTISTIC CHILDREN

THE TREATMENT OF psychotic-autistic children is problematic, for it is extremely difficult to establish contact with them. They are unable to maintain communication with others. They exclude themselves or are excluded by the nature of their condition from the reality and content of human relationship.

Most handicapped children respond readily to the individual music therapy situation. They become active and join the therapist in whatever way they can in music-making. The incapacities they reveal as they do this can be taken up and worked with directly through improvisation.

With the psychotic-autistic children in this project, this was rarely possible. For musical work on any functional disorder necessarily incurred the resistiveness inherent in an emotional pathology. In each child the one appeared as an expression of the other, and in the effort to secure an active musical contact we had to work variously round, through, and with the resistive manifestations of psychosis. Swings of behaviour came to be expected in the course of therapy as evoked or developing responses induced intercommunication.

* * *

With the more active children (these were in the minority), therapy followed a certain sequence of stages: The first was the gradual establishing of limited responsive activity during which fear or confusion was dispelled by the discovery of pleasure in the activity and the gaining of confidence in the therapy situation. From this stage, it became possible to develop individually specific forms of musical activity which heightened a child's interest and satisfaction and brought mobility into his response. This then led into an intensity of participation which could ultimately become personally self-expressive for a child. Such a process might be achieved in six months—it could take up to two years. The work with Rosita followed this course.

When she began music therapy in May 1962 Rosita was a dreamy, morose six-year-old, whose main preoccupation in life was knotting shoelaces or pieces of string into bizarre figures. Her speech was minimal and echolalic. She did not refer to herself as "I" or "me", but as "you", "she" or "her", or by her name. Her behaviour was erratic and unpredictable.

In her first session she sat by the piano and beat on a small drum. I accompanied her beating and tried to bring rhythmic variety into it to awaken her interest. With a frown on her face, as if this was all very strange to her, she would try to follow. She was not able to sustain this effort for long and would often revert to beating dreamily in tempi of her own or would sit and suck her thumb. But she was a musical child and after a month's consistent work of two ten-minute sessions weekly she had made considerable progress. Although she still looked puzzled, as if something was happening to her which she could not understand, she was able to be musically awakened. She beat simple rhythmic patterns as they were played, imitated accented beats, and made *accelerandi* with me. When her waltz-song "Rosita Can Say Hello" was introduced into the improvisation, she would not sing it, but she beat to it and smiled with pleasure.

Then followed an experience typical in work with autistic children: this promising development in her response ceased— she became regressed and her responses became negative. She had begun to enter into a rich and active exchange of experience, a state of arousal and communicativeness totally unfamiliar to her. The personality changes she felt stirring within her as a result of her engagement were confusing and threatening to her. The next five months were difficult. She did no consistent work and was as obstreperous as only she could be. She set up a pattern of evasion and teasing which became increasingly meaningless.

Finally, and quite unpredictably, in November we got her back to work by a tactic that was as bizarre as her behaviour. She was sitting far away from the piano. To dolorous music the assistant on an impulse approached her slowly backwards, and without turning around offered her the end of a drum-stick under his arm. She took it and in a docile manner, followed him to the drum and began to beat. This broke the habit of refusal; she rediscovered her pleasure in the activity and her musical interest took over. By the end of January, the sessions, once weekly, were twenty minutes long. She *worked* at the drum the whole time. The improvisations for her were full of vitality, with many changes and contrasts of tempo, dynamics, idiom, and emotional quality.

She initiated a musical game with me: she would stop beating, wait for me to stop too, and then begin to beat softly and slowly, watching me intently. I would improvise similarly with her until suddenly she would beat loudly with tremendous vigour—I immediately matched this in my playing. She enjoyed this game and it was repeated many times.

Most of Rosita's music was very stimulating; a kind of dissonant "carnival" waltz alternated with an idiom used with very few children—jazz. This musical material was subject to all kinds of developments and variations to keep Rosita fully awake and active (see photos Appendix I, 6). The turning point of the work came in a session in February. She was very eager that day and I was able to lead the improvisation, and Rosita with it, into a tremendously energetic *crescendo*. She began to exclaim rhythmically with the music and then to sing, intently but quietly, "Rosita can beat it, yes she can!"—the words of her jazzy song.

This was a breakthrough into *song*. After this the drum-beating diminished; it had served its purpose. We have found this to be a therapeutic milestone with many children. As their drum-beating becomes ever more expressive of musical-emotional involvement, they are propelled into new regions of expressive freedom. They simply cannot resist what is happening to them; they just have to sing!

Rosita became so at ease and communicative that many songs could be developed for her. She took these up as personal expressions and asked for them repeatedly, seeming to find a security of experience and relationship in them. At times she thoughtfully, softly improvised. We worked in this way until October 1963. During this period she began spontaneously to use the first-person pronouns, her vocabulary improved beyond all expectation, and psychiatrists working with her family reported considerable progress in her behaviour and responsiveness at home.

* * *

The investigational possibilities of music therapy based on improvisation proved to be an aid in differential diagnosis. Comparative experiences made it possible to discern in some children responses that indicated not so much autism as aphasia or brain-injury complicated by emotional disturbance. Such impressions were later borne out by the results of long-term treatment. The ability of the therapy to explore a child's personality and to pick up unrealized sensitivities and character attributes also contributed to prognosis. The case of David illustrates this.

David was a six-year-old who possessed the phenomenal ability to name the day on which any date would fall in this year, next year, or even the one after that. He was admitted to the Unit because of his symbiotic behaviour, chronic anxiety, and poor visual-motor coordination. However, we quickly found out that in music his *audio-motor* coordination was excellent.

One thing he did early in treatment impressed us deeply. He

was beating the drum when I led him into an *accelerando*. Many children become over-excited by this stimulating activity-experience. They are unable to stay with the music as it makes a gradual *accelerando*, but race ahead and beat as fast as they physically can. David too became excited and twice his beating began to run away with him, but both times he made a determined effort and regained control over himself. The *accelerando* was deliberately repeated many times. Each time he revealed his capacity to control himself, perceive what was musically required in the situation and attempt to accomplish it. We felt that this careful, caring response had revealed a most positive aspect of David's individuality, one that held a good prognosis. He also worked diligently to beat quite complex rhythmic patterns and melodic rhythms. He was immediately attentive to variations in dynamics, and sensitive to changes of tempo and to rubato. He had never done well in psychological tests, but he could accomplish exacting musical activities; his musical intelligence and perceptiveness were exceptional—and dependable.

David could not learn to tie his shoes. For nine months efforts had been made without success to teach him. When a student therapist put the process of tying a shoe into a song, David succeeded the second time through. Tying a shoe is always approached as a process involving spatial manipulation and visual control. David's visual-motor functions caused problems for him and generated anxiety. *A song is a form in time.* David had a special relationship to this element and could comprehend the shoe-tying process when it was organized in time through a song.

When he reached the age for leaving the Unit, the problem of placement arose. Were his intellectual possibilities limited by retardation or was his dysfunction psychological? Could he develop sufficient ego-strength to hold his own in life? In music therapy he had demonstrated intelligence, perceptiveness and stable qualities of ego-function. The positive report from music therapy supported his placement in an institution where good educational facilities and psychotherapy were available. Three years later his home life was becoming settled and he was attending junior high school one grade beyond his age level.

* * *

The younger or more severely autistic children rarely used the drum or cymbal in their early sessions. Therapy had to start by setting any habitual mode of behaviour or any fragmentary evoked response into a musical context. This was tenuous, searching work. Of great importance was the sustaining of mood through idiom— the creating of an emotional environment in which one could hope to stimulate and catch a response. Each child's responsiveness had to be nursed and taken in each session just as far as it could go. No external direction or demands were possible, especially in the early days of a course of therapy. The responses of Russell showed many features characteristic of this kind of work.

Russell began music therapy at the age of three-and-a-half. He was totally lacking in speech. Any changes in his surroundings, departure from routine, or the presence of a strange adult invoked extreme anxiety and often uncontrollable temper-tantrums. His physical development was still infantile; he would spend hours sitting on a chair, his legs drawn up under him, rocking rhythmically back and forth, half humming, half grunting.

In March 1963, some weeks after his admittance to the Unit, we created a special situation through which to introduce him to music therapy. Three children, to whom he was now accustomed, came to the music room with him. Arranged about the room were a variety of drums and cymbals, and a large wooden xylophone. The three children chose instruments and began to use them freely. I accompanied them and attempted to interrelate their activities by giving them musical meaning. Russell took the chair furthest from the piano, sat in his usual way and became inattentive to everything, withdrawing into the internal experience of his rocking. After some minutes the assistant slid Russell's chair over beside mine at the piano. By pitching his weight differently in his rocking, he immediately drove the chair backwards some three feet. I began to play in the tempo of his rocking—which also put his rhythmical grunts in time with the music. A few minutes later, rocking skilfully, he impelled his chair forwards and returned to the place beside me. For the next six weeks he came to music therapy once weekly with the other children and always sat in this place.

Very often I accompanied his rocking, for the most part gently playing and singing to him chant-like music, similar in style to Gregorian chant. His grunting became more and more musical in quality and he began to sound notes in the key of the improvisation, always in the rhythm of his rocking. His vocal responses appeared to be as inwardly experienced as his rocking, yet they were not so completely enclosed and automatous for they were related to the improvisation and often changed in emphasis with it. There was a meditative mood about Russell at this time; outwardly he seemed withdrawn but I sensed a musical awareness growing within him along with the delicate musical relationship we were then forming. I felt that this awareness was coming to consciousness within Russell as he "meditatively" experienced the sounding and answering of notes between us.

The three other children were active all this time and the improvisation was directed flexibly among them. Occasionally two of them, each at a large mounted orchestral cymbal, would start a kind of cymbal "duel", each seeing who could make the loudest *crescendo*. The room rang with cymbal tone at those times. Russell, who was said to be unable to tolerate loud noises, would look round with mild interest as if distracted from the internal experience in which he was engrossed.

After the summer recess we judged that he was sufficiently established in his musical experiences to come to therapy alone. The work continued as before. His vocal responses increased in range and in variety of musical inflection; they began to be free of his rocking. He would sustain notes and change pitch in response to my playing and singing. He still resisted strongly any change in his environmental routine and often cried or had a tantrum when removed from his particular day-care worker to come to music. As he was carried along the corridor to the music room, I would be improvising, creating a mood for the beginning of the session. As soon as he heard the music he would change the notes of his crying to harmonize with it. Once in the room and on his chair, fear would leave him and his crying became "singing".

After some weeks a time came when we felt Russell should do a little musical work. A very small drum and a xylophone, on which were set out three notes in the key of his music, were placed beside him. But he would not take up the beater to play them. This was part of his old pathological picture—something that had to break down or change if that which was newly-growing within him was to come out into expression. Hitherto my work with him had been gentle and undemanding; I now began to challenge this "old self" of Russell.

This was a critical thing to do to such a young, severely autistic child whose habits of behaviour were deeply ingrained. There was a danger that we would lose the ground we had gained, that he would panic and reject the entire situation. Yet we felt that he had to step on to a new plane of activity and experience, otherwise music therapy would not progress but degenerate into a form of musical coddling. Clinically, I sensed that I had by now a secure enough relationship to his awakening musical-emotional awareness to avert disaster. I disturbed his placid composure by deliberately provoking him.

His immediate reaction was to fly into a rage and yell, but his *new musical self* transformed rage into musical expression—he *sang* his rage, and I could sing with him my understanding of it and my contending attitude towards it. There were no words in this "duet": it was an intense exchange of held notes and short melodic-rhythmic phrases. Over a harmonic sequence of supporting chords our singing reached a climax. He clearly sang the melodic resolution and then became quiet. This expressed an *emotional resolution*—signifying the presence of some capability to accept a new direction of activity.

In all autistic children there appears a decided lack or distortion of ego-development, particularly in its relation to emotional life and the expressive acts that belong to it. This is so whether the autism is seen as purely traumatic in origin or if it has organic or aphasoid accompaniments. Through his responsive activity Russell was forming a new inner ego-organization—*inner* in the sense that it was developing within the distorted structure of his outer personality. It possessed its own budding emotional life and used, as its own instrument of expression, his singing voice. In the moment of challenge and rage this newly-developing ego-organization took hold of his old, turbulent emotional reactions and impressed upon them a responsive and organizing capacity. That he could do this and then go on to attain the musical resolution between us meant that the old wall of fear and of self-protection against the world had been breached *from within*. Russell's new ego-organization could now begin to express itself with a little freedom and pleasure. In the following sessions he took the beater that was offered to him and in a happy, infantlike exploration began to play upon the xylophone bars and the drum.

During these weeks I was also working to free him from the compulsion of his rocking. This was already diminishing, for careful changes of tempo in the improvisation could slow it down or speed it up. When syncopations were played against it he would either stop in confusion or rock harder. In the context of the syncopated rhythm, his efforts to maintain his rocking turned it into a more conscious musical-rhythmic expression. This externalized his experience of it.

As he became freer from this compulsion, he no longer

received his musical experiences in internal seclusion. His growing expressiveness was expanding his awareness to include me as the source of his music, the stimulator of his responses. It was now possible to stop his rocking by holding a note in my singing. The subduing of the rocking directly improved his use of the beater and often his beating showed the influence of rhythmic structures in the improvisations. All this was great progress for him and his parents were reported as saying in the spring of 1964: "Russell has developed a million-dollar smile!"

This, and his freer bearing in the sessions indicated that he had gained a new stage of development. We recognized how far he had progressed for such a young, severely ill child, and considered it wise to give him a rest. When intensive treatment results in some measure of self-realization a child often needs time to consolidate his new modes of function, time to equalize his development by spreading his new appreciations into the situations and activities of his life. Individual work with several children had suggested that the ego-organization of a child in therapy had an individual optimum rate of growth. It could not safely achieve more in a given time—and in a given situation—than was in its nature to achieve. This had to be respected in the special circumstances of individual therapy, for improvisational clinical work could be powerfully intrusive. If these facts were disregarded there could be the danger of placing insupportable stresses on a child, and hence of engendering confusion and instability where one should nourish and integrate. This could seriously injure a child's self-confidence.

Russell attended occasional group activities for a time. In September 1964 his individual therapy recommenced; within a month he was beating drum, cymbal and xylophone with determination and pleasure.

*　*　*

Because of the lack of previous inquiry in this field and the dearth of relevant information, it was inevitable that guidelines for research be determined empirically. The project being first and foremost a treatment project, no attempt was made to standardize musical stimuli in order to obtain a restricted orientation of response; all data resulting from creative clinical work had to be accepted as significant. An extensive amount of diverse data was yielded in a variety of interconnected phenomena. In behavioural response: motoric and vocal activity, psychological activation, and developmental trends. In music the impact of: idiom, thematic material, rhythmic structure, and expressive components. All became factors in a network of experience requiring differentiation and interpretation. The sheer range of the phenomena necessitated a broadly based, unbiased approach to research.

As the project proceeded research separated into three areas:

1. *Clinical Methodology:* working concepts; improvisational resources; analysis of causative factors in music; therapeutic principles and techniques.
2. *Interpretative Studies:* psychology and neurology of musical responses; musically-activated ego-functions; personality development; relationships between song and speech; case studies.
3. *Evaluation.* Rating-scales covering: child-therapist relationship; qualities of resistiveness; modes and intensities of communication; vocal responses and motoric-rhythmic activities assessed in terms of the structural and expressive musical components they contained.

Study and delineation continued in all areas of research after the termination of the N.I.M.H. grant in 1967. Subsequently the project was transferred to the Child Study Centre of Philadelphia. A comprehensive report on the project, and a statement of its findings will appear in a manual on individual therapy based on improvisation, to be published by the John Day Company, Publishers, New York.

November 1962—March 1967

School District of Philadelphia, Board of Public Education. *Approximately 450 Retarded Trainable children* (I.Q. 20–50), age 7 to 16, 40 Retarded Educable children† (I.Q. 50–75), age 11 to 15, in group activities.*

In June 1962, two Associate Superintendents of the School District of Philadelphia in charge of Curriculum and Teacher Training, observed individual therapy and a Pif-Paf-Poltrie *session at the Day-Care Centre for Autistic Children, University of Pennsylvania. They became convinced that a music therapy programme would have great value in the then newly-instituted classes for the Retarded Trainable in the city's schools. A programme was planned with two main objectives: one was to demonstrate through work with the children that they were capable of response to an active approach and of development as a result—this was to help animate the entire programme for the trainable; the other was to give instruction in music therapy techniques to interested, capable personnel. This project, under the Department of Special Education, was conducted concurrently with the N.I.M.H. Project with Autistic Children; up until June 1966, three days weekly were spent in the schools.*

The materials and methods developed originally at Sunfield Children's Home and further refined in group activities at the Devereux Schools and the Institute of Logopedics, were used

* Severely Subnormal.
† Educationally Subnormal.

extensively. New compositions were continuously developed, all materials being graded in complexity and intensity to provide the possibilities for meaningful participation across a wide range of ability. On-going work was observed by all teachers of trainable children. Most of the children possessed good musical intelligence; in many it was surprisingly advanced. Therapy depended on engaging this musical intelligence as fully as possible, drawing each child into concentrated activity. The results observed with trainable children were the growth of emotional maturity and social competence with concomitant gains in: perceptivity, ability to concentrate, attention-span, self-confidence and satisfaction in achievement, improvement in speech, and a lessening of withdrawal and of other emotional handicaps.

During 1963–64, a pilot demonstration project was conducted with Retarded Educable children. They were mostly Negro, and from an underprivileged section of the city. The musical activities for these children needed to be more advanced, the demands made upon them and their resulting achievements commensurate with their more realized abilities. The tenor of the work was very different, for although the Educable participate in "normal" life to a far greater extent than the Trainable, they are rarely able to function with ease and satisfaction, and so live with inner or outer conflict. This project demonstrated that music therapy was able to free these children from the frustrations and tensions that bedevilled their lives. Improvements in classroom attitudes and behaviour resulted in the upgrading of several children's teachability. Withdrawn or hostile children were brought effectively into the group. Even more far-reaching were changes in social conduct outside the school.

Many of the Educable children appeared to develop, through their participation in the work of the groups as a whole, a new self-image. This was directly nourished by the quality of the emotional experience all had received, strengthened by the purposefulness they had used, and illumined by the happiness of their achievements. There had to be a high standard of artistic quality in the music they worked with. This was not merely for reasons of aesthetic taste, but because the emotional and psycho-moral content of such music is so much more developmentally effective. Few compositions exist which can make the right impact at the right depth for children of this kind—and yet which lie within their musical abilities. For this project special works were composed. These comprised settings of ten poems from Prayers from the Ark *by Carmen de Gasztold, for piano, singers and instrumentalists, and a setting of the 23rd Psalm for piano, singing chorus, speech chorus, and an instrumentalist.*

Educable children gave three public performances at the end of this project; the Trainable gave performances of a nativity play every Christmas, instrumental concerts annually, and several demonstrations to professional audiences.

A successful demonstration of Play-songs *and* Pif-Paf-Poltrie *was given with normal kindergarten children for all the kindergarten teachers in the school system; lectures on musical activities followed for these teachers.*

A second team of therapists, Dr and Mrs Herbert Levin, was engaged and trained to increase the coverage of the music therapy programme for the Trainable. Later these therapists also gave demonstrations with emotionally disturbed and with physically-handicapped children. Felice Wolmut, a music therapist and voice teacher, joined the staff for a year to work with Trainable children specifically on speech and behaviour problems by means of singing.

During 1963 and '64, teachers of the Trainable were instructed in music therapy techniques under working conditions. Ultimately, teachers in several schools were chosen by their principals and co-workers for training in teamwork. Special funds were raised to equip the four largest centres with sets of selected instruments.

In 1965 and '66, working sessions were filmed for demonstration and training purposes; in 1967 instructional manuals were prepared for teachers; Herbert and Gail Levin assumed responsibility for the entire project. They continued treatment and teacher training, and formed an All-City Orchestra in which the most musical children from all the Trainable centres could rehearse and perform advanced instrumental compositions written by Herbert Levin.

VIII

GROUP MUSICAL ACTIVITIES WITH TRAINABLE CHILDREN

THE PROJECT WAS first based in a school containing just four classes of Trainable children, ten in a class. This made an ideal demonstration centre. The ages of the children, from seven to sixteen, gave scope for developing activities emotionally suitable to different age-levels. There was a mixture of pathologies typical of groups of Trainable children: brain-injury with different behavioural effects, a variety of conditions among mongoloid children, different degrees of emotional disturbance, a proportion of cases manifesting cerebral palsy, and speech handicaps from mild to severe. The children therefore presented varied qualities of responsiveness, and the range of their conditions enabled us to get children with different pathologies to work together so that their capacities could supplement each other—the abilities of one supporting the deficiencies of another. Very few of the children had previously experienced any intensive treatment or educational programme. There were equal numbers of Negro and white children.

The facilities of the school were excellent for the project. The music room was a large classroom that could hold groups of up to twenty-five comfortably with plenty of room for movement. A great asset was the moderately-sized auditorium, in which all the children and teachers could gather for singing. Its simple stage could be used for plays and larger instrumental ensembles. The acoustics of the auditorium were favourable— an important consideration in group musical activities: there was sufficient reverberation to vivify the tones of voices and instruments without any prolonged echoing to blur melodic phrases or harmonic progressions.

The smallness of the staff made it possible to conduct the project flexibly. With the cooperation of the four teachers, daily schedules could be arranged to accommodate the immediate objectives of music therapy, and children could be taken selectively out of their classes whenever it was necessary to make up special groups to suit particular needs and abilities.

In the first two days of the project we introduced several *Play-songs* to all the children, and *Pif-Paf-Poltrie* was done with the two younger groups. Then, to gain a more direct insight into the children, we explored their reactions when drum-beating to piano improvisations. Each class was taken separately, the children coming up in turn for five minutes work at the drum and cymbal. Both improvisation and the songs they had sung or heard were used. Each child's response was explored to the limit of its musical ability: basic beating, tempo mobility and sensitivity to rhythmic patterns, melodic rhythms, dynamics and phrase structure were all used as testing criteria. From close observation of the children at work and the analysis of the recordings made, we gained a clear impression of the condition and character of each child and also direct information about his inherent musical responsiveness. In this way we obtained practical indications for immediate work.

These findings were discussed and confirmed with the teachers and the first objectives of the project outlined. It was agreed that in the musical activities class control should be flexible, the children being given the freedom to express their responses and to develop their own feelings for what belonged constructively to a situation. It was also agreed that no child's difficulties should be discussed in his hearing.

During the first two weeks we concentrated on *Play-songs* and *Pif-Paf-Poltrie* with all classes. To fulfil one main aim of the project—that it should demonstrate the developmental capabilities of Trainable children, summaries of and comments on the course of each day's work were made for the Curriculum and Teacher Training offices. An excerpt from the summary of *November 16, 1962*, reports:

We began the day's work with class 3. Eddie had been Pif-Paf on Wednesday. Today, Charles was enthusiastic to take the part. The game went well, the children being co-operative and anticipating the parts they took. When it came to the sweeping, the job was really very big for Charles and he had to learn how to control himself as he worked. To begin with he went at it too quickly and in a scattered way. Then he settled down and became more methodical and diligent. His poor vision hindered him and often leaves escaped his sweeping. The other children helped him by quietly calling his attention to them.

At 10.30 an assembly was held. A number of visitors from the administration building had arrived to observe. We separated boys and girls, sat them on opposite sides of the centre aisle and started with antiphonal singing. The children were soon singing with pep and pleasure. We used all the songs previously taught. Children also came up to the piano individually to sing *What Shall We Do with the Dog?* as a solo. Each soloist could choose the animal he or she wanted to sing about and everyone would make the sound of that animal when the time came in the song. This was enthusiastically received and there were more requests to be the solo singer than we had time for. This kind of activity gives the children pleasure and satisfaction, and yet there is much more to it than entertainment. The experience of singing such a song to his schoolmates gives the soloist an experience of himself in action and he can begin to learn some positive things about his own abilities. As the children watch, listen, and sing back to each other, they begin to get clearer, more differentiated experiences of each other. If the soloist is really trying, out of his own wish, his very own initiative, then those who watch will sooner or later become aware of this. This creates morale and the kind of group mood which builds good social relationships.

Following the assembly we took class 2, and after singing a new song composed to greet the children as they entered the music room, began another *Pif*. We had asked the visitors to sit with the children, to join them in the singing and actions, and always to keep their attention upon the child who was the focus of the activity at any given moment. Larry made a careful Pif. It is most interesting to us to see this game work with these children as we have seen it work with so many others in other situations. Many of the children, as one sees them in a classroom or in any everyday situation, give a misleading picture of themselves. All too often one sees what the world has made of them and not what they could have become if their inherent resources for growth had been activated. You see the compromise they have made with life—or the compromise that life has been prepared to accept from them. For example, you see the sad, handicapped child who can only be a kind of clown, or the high-grade mongoloid girl with a set of conditioned but empty responses. We find *Pif-Paf-Poltrie* gets behind all this and arouses the deep interest of the essential individuality. We begin to see another side of the children, and it is this side that we wish to activate and develop.

* * *

With the approach of Christmas we envisaged a Christmas play performed by the children. The idea was unanimously approved at a parent-teachers' meeting, and household materials and discarded clothing for costumes were promised.

The tableau of *The Friendly Animals* that had been enacted at the Institute of Logopedics the previous year, was taken as the principal theme. Around this a complete nativity play was evolved. The speech, action, and structure were determined in practical work with the children. Familiar Christmas carols were chosen which the audience could sing while the children portrayed the principal scenes.

In experimental work in the classroom using a variety of Indian bells, and horns, cymbals, a tambourine and a triangle, an orchestra of 10 children was formed. It was to play, with the piano, specially composed music consisting of an Overture, descriptive passages to accompany the entrances and other actions of the characters in the play, and a Finale.

December 12. Orchestral rehearsal. After the three previous sessions in the music room we moved to the auditorium to rehearse under performance conditions. The orchestra is positioned over to one side immediately next to the stage. A platform for the players has been arranged around the piano. This will enable them to see the play better and to be seen by the audience. It also creates a setting for the orchestra which emphasizes its special role and gives the players a sense of unity.

We worked over the music for the whole play and added extra bells for the Finale, *Christmas Bells*. The rehearsals are now slowed down because some of the children who were in the orchestra last week are ill and we have to take time to teach the discipline of orchestral ensemble to new players. Most of the children are used to beating or shaking instruments indiscriminately to recordings and it takes a little time to free them of this notion of music-making. But as this is achieved, each child in his own time grows into the new experience of selective, ordered playing making definite pieces of music. The growth of awareness, pleasure and mutual appreciation that takes place among the children is beautiful to see.

* * *

None of the children taking parts in the play had ever been

involved in such a thing before. A few had vague ideas of what performance meant; most could have no conception of it at all. Gradually, in the day-to-day work, sections of the action were established. During these days the children were arriving in the school buses laden with bags and boxes of donated materials for costumes. Teachers and bus matrons worked at dyeing, fitting and sewing costumes. Masks were made for the Friendly Animals. A mood of excitement began to fill the school.

December 13. Teachers' meeting. Discussed the plans for the day, the progress of the play and the children's responses. We talked with the teachers and the principal about our hopes and intentions—that in producing this play we wanted to create an experience for the children, a rich and many-sided experience. We described how this was being built, step by step, bringing together acting, speech, music and costumes. We stressed how essential it was that as we worked with the children we believed in what we were doing; and that everyone actively involved in this experience should share this attitude. For this *creative attitude* would arouse and sustain the children's enthusiasm; it would engender the right mood for the play.

* * *

The children in the orchestra and the cast were now sufficiently familiar with their parts to be able to rehearse together. As the playing of the orchestra added the moods of the music to the sequence of the action, the whole organization of the play became clear and its dramatic content came through. Most of the actors began to show an increasing enjoyment of the scenes and a feeling for their parts. Some were surprisingly observant and retentive. The clarity of the play's situations stimulated their ability to comprehend them, and out of comprehension to take on responsibility.

The day before the performance the dress rehearsal was held and final production details settled. It was most important to ensure that the functions of the four supporting teachers were absolutely clear so that the children's giving of the play would be competently, unobtrusively served.

December 20. Performance. A large audience of relatives, friends, and officials of the school district filled the auditorium. The performance was an adventure at every moment. The children achieved their first experience of giving a play. The presence of the audience took the play out of ours and the teachers' hands, made it the children's, and set them on a level of performance. Their responses to this were all individual: some were very conscious of being on this level and tackled the challenge of it; many had a great deal of pleasure; others took pride in their parts; some were fearful. All knew we were there to sustain and lead if necessary. They watched each other and waited for cues. The feeling of cooperative *mutual effort* was really strong. The players and instrumentalists were most warmly applauded. Afterwards there was a wonderful feeling of festivity and attainment.

The therapeutic effects of such play-producing with Trainable children are many-sided and potentially far-reaching. During the rehearsals the children live in the evolving production. They learn new activities, new words, new music. They attend to each other's efforts, and see handicaps being overcome. They gain more positive experiences of each other and of themselves. They learn how to take a role. They have the excitement of being fitted with and wearing costumes. The total activity is stimulating. It is also hard work for them and because it is hard work they take it seriously. It lifts them out of the ruts they have settled into and creates a new interest and purpose which can become each child's own, something to be happy about, something to anticipate and to believe in.

In the rehearsals the practice of self-control and responsiveness to each other induces awareness. This can blossom in the performance into a valuable feeling of self-confidence. The effects of the performance will be felt by each child personally; if his role is an attainment for him, he will certainly know it. Most children will have to make a special effort to play their parts and when they sense the quality of the audience's attention, and that they are giving pleasure to, or stirring the audience, they will feel satisfaction. Also, the play and the players are a unity; through their efforts they carry the play, while its action carries and expresses them. When the content of the play is realized and it meets with appreciation, the children are fulfilled.

The relationship between children and teachers can be deepened in building a play. Teachers have the opportunity to allow a child's initiative to develop. Instead of approaching him instructionally, they work with him artistically. This enables him to show more of his individuality in action. Instead of being continually concerned with the child's intellectual impairment—and of subjecting him, all too often, to negative experiences—teachers can gain knowledge of his capacity for feeling, of his imagination, of his attitude, and of his sensitivity to the feelings of others. Hitherto unsuspected abilities present themselves for classroom work.

The effects of the play can also reach into a child's family life. When the results of his development through the rehearsals are expressed in the way he plays his part in the performance, his parents can see him in a new light. They see him achieve an individual quality of independence. The tension and concern they usually feel about their child's condition can be eased by their experience of his commitment to the play's action. They share in his enjoyment and become proud of him in his success. That this happens in a positive, social event centred on what all the children do together, helps to break down the isolation many parents of handicapped children feel.

* * *

After the Christmas vacation all the children were given another short drum-beating/improvisational exploration. Two facts of great interest emerged. One was that every child who had manifested a particular impairment in the previous exploration—and almost all had—showed the *tendency to beat in exactly the same form of disorder*. This confirmed that each child's original mode of beating was in no way accidental but was a genuine expression of pathology, a kind of signature of condition. The second fact of interest was that within their individual modes of activity, perhaps three-quarters of the children showed signs of *gains in organization and freedom of response*, including *all* the children who had taken part in the play.

In February the internal demonstration aspect of the project commenced. The teachers in the school system with classes of Trainable children came in groups of four to the demonstration centre to spend three days observing the music therapy programme. Principals and supervisors from each school district also attended. As we were by this time also working with the instruments, songs and speech of *The Three Bears*, the visitors could observe a variety of activity. Discussions were held after the working sessions referring to what the teachers had seen. These led into considerations of pathology, children's musical responsiveness, and the aims and techniques of music therapy.

The school system's programme for Trainable children was in its relatively early days and it became our function to advance concepts of therapy to educationally-oriented workers. In the years before the school system admitted Trainable children as such, it could always approach those categories of children unable to participate in the regular education programme—the physically disabled, the behaviourally disturbed, the slow learners, etc.—as being basically educational problems. But for Trainable children this approach had no meaning and could not provide a basis for devising an effective curriculum for them.

We stressed the fact that the teachers were not just handling severe learning and behaviour problems, but were working with children suffering from *pathologies*; and that although each child's present state of development showed the arrest or distortions caused by mental and emotional dysfunctions, this was not a condition of hopeless limitation. For the children could be aroused through special forms of experience in which they could participate. When these were sustained, therapeutic processes could be set in motion and led onward to achieve definite, positive gains in development. The key idea needing clarification was the idea of *experience*. Only through the creation of suitable experiences could the latent developmental forces in mentally handicapped children be drawn into effect. Such experiences had to be stimulating, meaningful and possess emotional character. They also had to invite the participation of children and integrate it so that it could be significant both for the individual's involvement and the group's interactivity.

Several directives for classroom work that were then current were confusing many teachers and inhibiting their own constructive impulses. These were to the effect that a kind of babysitting attitude was realistic with Trainable children—they were brain-injured, could not learn, could not help their behaviour, and it would be unkind and unreasonable to challenge them in any way; they were incapable of performing more than one simple action at a time; their memories were weak; they were unable to concentrate on anything for longer than fifteen minutes.

The music therapy activities were demonstrating that these tenets were just not true. When challenge was meaningful and presented in a productive activity, the children were able to meet it. They could do more than one activity at a time—children were learning to play instrumental parts while they watched the leader's directing, watched and listened to each other's playing, and sang as they played. They were holding in their memories the words and melodies of over twenty songs, the structure of *Pif-Paf-Poltrie*, and precise instrumental parts. Working sessions on *The Three Bears* often lasted fifty minutes or more with no diminution of concentration.

All through the spring months, during the observation programme, *The Three Bears* was progressively built up with the three younger classes. As this was an already completed composition we had a certain problem. This was to present it to the children in such a way *that their responses would re-create it*— that they could in consequence identify themselves through their involvement with as much of its experience as possible. Then we would not be merely teaching them its parts to prepare them for performance.

The composition divided into sixteen main sections of musical activity, consisting of instrumental playing, singing, and rhythmical speech. These either connected directly or were linked by narrative and short instrumental passages. A sequence of three sections formed the dramatic core of the composition— *The Birds' Song*, with its four bird-calls; *The Bears' House*, a descriptive passage of antiphonal rhythmic speech supported by music; and *The Bears' Song*, with the 'cello and two violins. This sequence was introduced first in order to create a nucleus of music and ideas.

To enliven the children's experience, a large picture was drawn with coloured chalks in the music room. It portrayed the Bears in and around their house and garden, and the Birds in the woods. Every concept in the three musical sections was illustrated. The teachers in the demonstration centre took up this scene and worked with it in their classrooms. The children made pictures of the house and the characters, spontaneously using the words of the songs and speech to describe them. In two weeks this nucleus of experience was firmly established. The musical sections preceding it and those that developed the story further could then be linked successively to it. With each new character or development of the action, a new song, an instrument, or a speech passage appeared. The work became a musical adventure.

Every song with instrumental parts was used repeatedly with each class. Usually we worked with the more capable children first so that those who were slower to grasp the form of the activity or who were too afraid of failure to have the courage to try, might learn from them.

February 27, 1963. It was a revelation to see what Donald, Rickie, Beth and Allen—all severely handicapped—had absorbed by watching and listening. They were serious when they came to play and maintained an active attentiveness for an impressively long time. Sarah is becoming more happy and willing to participate. She is a perceptive, sensitive, high-grade mongoloid who has been seriously robbed of self-confidence. She played Baby Bear well, but when she came to play the Cuckoo she was trembling and tense. It was a most important step for her that today she was able to endure the failures of her first attempts and to keep on trying. Her shoulder-shrugging, head-averting "don't bother me" re-action, with which she protects herself from intimidating situations was certainly there, but there was something else— a love of the activity and some feeling of security in it. Because of this we were able to bring her through her extreme nervousness and she performed the Cuckoo with rhythmic accuracy. She showed real pleasure.

* * *

The instruments, with their different characters and authentic musical sounds, made a prodigious impact upon the children; everyone was eager to handle them and play them—they were treated with care and affection as if they were living friends. As the composition began to grow, a wave of excited anticipation, a kind of hunger for experience and participation swept through the three classes.

For the older children—the fourth class—we felt a different character of experience was needed and at first we worked experimentally with them. Because there was a sad heaviness about many of the children we tried out the idea of developing a humorous play. But it soon became evident that they could have no real point of contact with such a play and that they needed a more dramatic and gripping activity. We acquired a number of different sized, variously toned Korean, Taiwanese, Indian and Kenyan drums and began to evolve a carefully-controlled drum ensemble. As a structural basis the rhythmic patterns of speech phrases were used, and the children beat them solo, in succession and in chorus—both antiphonally and in unison with the piano. Variations in tempo and dynamics were introduced expressively. Cymbals and a gong were added for interest and colour. The piano improvisations were symphonic in quality. Gradually the work took a dramatic form. Several specific drums became characters, each with a different mood—one was angry, another sad, etc. The music and its rhythms expressed these emotions. A drum chorus supported and answered each solo drum part.

Together with both the on-going instrumental works, *Pif-Paf-Poltrie* was used weekly with each class and new *Play-songs* were introduced when the children were ready for them. Because of the close, mutual effort involved and the warmth and fun of the activities, many children—particularly the younger ones—were very demonstrative at the end of the sessions. In the informality of relationship in the music room, we responded with equal affection. This also was an innovation for the educational structure.

April 5. This week one of the visiting teachers made a comment about the affection we show and give to the children. Some teachers were of the opinion that affection should not be expressed in so direct a way. We explained that music is an emotionally awakening experience for the children and that often they are spontaneously moved to come and embrace us to express their happiness. The work is also so intimately involved in the children's personality growth that they feel a special closeness to us. They naturally want to express this and it would be a denial of our relationship with them if we were to set up alien limits to behaviour. We are, after all, working in a child's world—a special child's world. Admittedly, there are circumstances where physically expressed affection could lead to awkward situations, but each situation should be handled individually out of practical experience. We do not consider it possible in therapy with these children to lay down regulations for conduct.

* * *

Many teachers were warmly appreciative of the music therapy programme. They found in the activeness of the approach and the children's responses, encouragement for their own classroom work. Practical indications for group-leading and piano-playing were given whenever requested.

Early in May, *The Three Bears* was approaching completion and a working session was televised from an educational studio. This was the first television programme in the city to show Trainable children at work and represented a rewarding achievement for the school system's public relations department. At the end of the month a "Spring Concert" for an audience of parents and teachers was given at the demonstration centre. The programme consisted of several *Play-songs*, a complete performance of *The Three Bears*, and the evolving drum work with the older class which was entitled *Work in Progress*.

By this time we had worked with every child consistently for seven months and could see how differently the musical activities were affecting different age groups.

June 5. There are many different sides to the personality-building effects of music therapy. For example, with older children it is possible in favourable circumstances to effect a rebirth of hopefulness, of self-confidence, and a revaluation of the feeling and meaning of self and of life's meaning. The clouds of resignation that darken the lives of so many of the older children can be dispelled, at least to some degree. We try to rectify the effects of any neglect or misunderstanding they may have experienced and to compensate for the lack of fulfilment that life must necessarily hold for them.

The character of therapy with younger children is quite different, for they are involved—in varying degrees of intensity and in quite individual ways—in processes of inner differentiation and growth. Their personalities are in a fluid condition of "becoming" and their responses to the work spring from the changing ground of growing appreciation and skill. The character of their involvement modulates as their capacities develop and achieve new outlets. As one works with them one can often feel this internal growth in process in the way they use the structures and contents of the activities to further their self-realization.

* * *

Throughout these months the teachers of the children at the demonstration centre, who had been collaborating most closely with us, were observing—and working with—changes in the children's behaviour in the classrooms which were directly linked to music therapy. As the children's consciousness became more focused their attention-span was continually lengthening. Self-confidence was resulting from self-realization. Communication between the children and between them and the teachers increased. The use of speech was stimulated and behaviour problems tended to diminish, while life for the children—and also for those who worked with them at school and lived with them at home—appeared to become more fulfilled and progressive. Individual modes of response and progress among the children were highly personal, and the various flowerings of personality in many children were exhilarating and deeply stirring to observe.

IX

A RATIONALE OF GROUP MUSIC THERAPY

FOR A FURTHER year the music therapy programme in the School District of Philadelphia was concentrated at the demonstration centre. The project with Retarded Educable children was conducted; a different cast of Trainable children repeated *The Children's Christmas Play*; younger, initially less capable children took up *The Three Bears*; the drum work with the older Trainable group became *A Message for the King*, a rhythmically complex, dramatic composition for thirteen instrumentalists, singing chorus, narrator and pianist—Educable girls sang the vocal part at its performance in the 1964 Spring Concert. Thereafter the scope of the project was widened to provide a music therapy service for every centre for Trainable children in the city.

The working schedule was arranged to cover the centres in rotation, time being apportioned to each according to the number of its classes. The work in each centre came to have a distinct quality; this was determined by the racial composition of its population, the children's pathologies, the character of the neighbourhood, and by the spirit of the professional staff. Most of the group activities previously demonstrated were used. To suit the special needs of various groups, new songs and shorter instrumental works were composed by both music therapy teams and experimental resonator-bell activities were developed.

The effectiveness of the programme in each centre was enhanced when its teachers came to appreciate the part music therapy could play in their children's lives. This ensured that the children's enthusiasm was warmly accepted, their interest encouraged, and their achievements in therapy valued. A positive relationship would then form between the music therapy programme and the daily school life in which developments initiated in the one were brought to fruition in practical activities and social relationships in the other. The resulting rise in everyone's morale fed back directly into the music sessions and increased the whole-heartedness with which the children participated. When such a beneficial circle of events arose, the educational-therapeutic efficiency of the total milieu was greatly increased.

To facilitate such a working cooperation the following rationale of music therapy was prepared and distributed:

SCHOOL DISTRICT OF PHILADELPHIA
DEPARTMENT OF SPECIAL EDUCATION

MUSIC THERAPY PROGRAMME
FOR CHILDREN IN THE
RETARDED TRAINABLE CLASSES

AIMS . . . METHODS . . . ROLE IN SPECIAL EDUCATION

IT IS THE aim of the music therapy programme to help those children who are classified as Retarded Trainable to live better lives. We have found that music is a way of entering into the personalities of these children. Our techniques and methods are designed to help develop their potential and to strengthen the positive functions of their psyches. If we can be instrumental in doing this, then we can assist the children to build more developed personalities and to partake to their optimum in school life.

Work with Musical Instruments
We use a wide variety of simple musical instruments. The

children find these attractive and want to play them. This gives us the opportunity to bring children into purposeful activity and to heighten their awareness.

Most of the children we work with have serious mental dysfunctions; they cannot think abstractly. This part of their conscious life is shrouded in uncertainty. But as music is not an abstract activity for them, their experience of it is not confused; they can perceive music, learn it and remember it. Their egos can become freely active in musical experience and they can show inherent perceptiveness and intelligence in musical activities. These properties of music and musical activity we can use to strengthen the personalities of handicapped children.

Our instrumental works are designed to fulfil many requirements, for in working with groups of children we must serve a variety of needs. One child may need stimulation, another organization, a third may need to be given confidence, a fourth stand in need of challenge. Whatever the requirements, we work flexibly to meet them through and within active musical experience.

Working in this way we invite and hold the children's attention, then intensify their capacity for concentration. They begin to *work*. Through their purposeful activity a larger experience grows in which their combined efforts are integrated.

The different instrumental parts written for the children to play possess different dramatic-emotional qualities; they call for different levels of mental awareness and for greater or lesser degrees of physical dexterity. As each child begins to work with us we try to place him in the part that is most suited to his abilities or to his needs. Then, as the work becomes established, we can often move him from a simple part to one that is more demanding, one that was beyond his capacities when he began. In this way, children who have had little chance in life to free and integrate their capacities, are given opportunities to develop and progress. Under these special circumstances the children can act with decisiveness and pleasure;

they can discover the experiences of exercising alertness, thoughtfulness, self-control, and responsibility.

Song and Speech

The development of speech is a cardinal factor in the building of the personality as a whole. In forming psychic energy into words and thoughts, and into the verbal communications that sustain human relationships, a child structures his thought-life and his inner world of feelings that together make up a large part of his personality. Where speech is absent or impaired, this interaction with the environment does not take place correctly and the child remains communicatively unstimulated. He fails to mature emotionally and ego-development remains suspended. These conditions are encountered among children in classes for the Trainable throughout the city.

In songs there lies a direct means of stimulating verbal expression and the mental-emotional life that is connected with it. Therefore, when we work with singing we aim to keep the children as awake as possible to what they are doing. The songs we bring them contain ideas they can make their own. We often use antiphonal singing to arouse interaction in their songs, to engage their listening and to give purpose to their singing. Children enjoy a melody when it not merely carries the words along but expresses their meaning clearly and aptly. Dissonant harmonies are used to give life to the melodies and to emphasize important words.

The rhythms in which the words are set to music are essentially the same as those in which they would be spoken. This makes them more natural to sing. Speech phrases are set to melodic phrases that follow and tonally emphasize the natural intonations of speech. This enhances the expressive qualities of the children's voices, for much of the meaning of speech and the pleasure we take in using it lie in the musical inflection with which we speak. This is close to song and, particularly in children, expresses inner attitudes and feelings.

Very often it is in our emotions that the urge arises most strongly to communicate—to share our experiences with others. For this reason, in group singing we attempt to evoke a wide range of emotional experience and mood through the songs we present. We appeal to the children's emotions, so that their feelings will come to life and expression as they sing. They can then actively identify with the words they are singing. Verbal-vocal consciousness is intensified and focused, and the ego-activity that takes expression in language is strengthened.

Singing is a direct expression of the ego living simultaneously in its emotional life, its mental life, and in its physical vocal apparatus. Singing is one of the most integrated and, at the same time, one of the most intimate and telling of our expressive acts. A strong impression can be gained of a mentally handicapped child's inner condition from the way in which he sings. In working therapeutically with the defects or limitations in his singing, much can be done for him that has deep psychological significance.

Special Forms of Group Activity

Every human being develops through his experiences of, and his responses to life around him. What he finds in his experiences, what meanings they have for him, determine first his responses and then his development. The development of severely mentally handicapped children is confined because their contact with the world is limited by the pathologies they bear. Each child is cut off from life to a considerable extent; a great deal of his potential for personality development cannot be reached through the normal channels of education. Frequently his perceptive and interpretive capacities are further inhibited by emotional complications that increase the handicap he suffers.

In our group works we aim to create special forms of experience in which as many children as possible can find intensive purpose and meaning. Outwardly these works may appear to be removed from what is generally regarded as external reality. This is because we are creating, with clinical intention, quite specific situations in which we can work directly upon the ego-functions and other psychological capacities of the children.

Pif-Paf-Poltrie is such an activity. When we work with *Pif*, it becomes a world in itself. Yet it is not a "world apart" when the children carry its effects out into their daily lives. *The Three Bears* and *A Message for the King* similarly hold within their structures special modes of experience; in both, dramatic content and musical performance are used to integrate the children's capabilities.

Just because these works are so self-contained and complete the children can commit themselves to them with confidence. In them they find a total structure they can grasp and in which they can be active. The music arouses them, the activities engage their interest, and they adopt the meaning or fulfilment of the work as their own. This is a source of internal stimulation and great security to each child. He takes an increasing pleasure in his own activities and in those of his friends. The psychological freedom he gains supports a growing feeling of self-confidence. This is *subjectively sound* because it rests on his own developing capacities, and *objectively true* in that it results from an action well and successfully done in fellowship with others. This is a social experience of the greatest importance.

Music Therapy and the Classroom Teacher

The success of this music therapy project requires that all work be done in a spirit of mutual understanding and cooperation with the principals, supervisors, and teachers working with Retarded Trainable children. It is impossible to overestimate the importance of the role of the teacher and the responsibility she bears in her classroom work. Each day she must cope with a tremendous range of pathological complexes. She must work positively with the intricacies and variations of organic impairment. Emotional complications, emotional immaturity or confusion in the children limit their responses to her work. Restricted and/or distorted ego-development is present in almost every child. The teacher is involved in responsibilities deeper than academic and behavioural training.

It is the music therapists' role to supplement the educational and classroom activities of the teacher with a programme aimed at providing special experiences that have central psychological significance for the children, and which can be therapeutic for their whole development. The strengthening of ego-function, the liberation from emotional restrictions and the alleviation of behavioural problems, all make for happier, more fulfilled children who can participate more fully in their school life and derive greater benefit from it.

X

EPILOGUE:
TO THE MUSICIAN THERAPIST

Music is a world. Every one of us has his own experiences in that world. There are endless depths, infinite varieties and facets of musical experience for the listener, the student, the performer, the composer, and for the therapist.

Those whose pleasure it is to listen to music can derive various kinds of emotional and ideational experiences from the music they choose to hear. The music student, as he acquires his skills, has experiences that continually change and deepen as he progresses from composition to composition and learns the works of the great composers. The performer of music never ceases to discover and to understand more about the music he re-creates—no matter how often he performs it. The composer has still other experiences: in his study of music he is especially concerned with each composer's imaginative and creative use of melody, harmony and rhythm, with compositional techniques, structural innovations and with the relationship of content to form. He must know all this if he wishes the music he composes to have an organic connection with the musical achievements of the past. The composer has the experiences of the student, the listener, and usually of the performer, as well as those of his own creative work.

A musician who makes the decision to enter music therapy will have had many of these experiences, but once he begins to work as a *therapist* he will find new dimensions, new horizons and depths in the *art of music itself* rather than in musical compositions. What he discovers when he experiences the art of music as therapy will shed new light for him on all music.

To improvise or compose for handicapped children, to arrange music and play for them, becomes a totally new world of musical experience. The therapist may be musically very knowledgeable, he may have performed often, or have composed much music, yet now music becomes revitalized for him, completely changed in purpose and realization. All the compositional styles evolved during the last seven centuries, all the folk music, the idioms, the elements of music, the very notes themselves—even the smallest expressive and structural components—become significant in countless, undreamed-of ways. The world of music opens anew, now disclosing an inner musical life of therapeutic potential. The therapist feels reborn in his new musical-therapeutic experiences and realizes that the art of music as therapy will never cease to challenge him, never cease to require all his musical resources. As a mediator of therapeutic music he assumes new, uplifting responsibilities. Out of his love for music he approaches handicapped children musically, *feels* them musically. Through his practical ability as a musician he works with them clinically. With his musical perceptiveness and musical intelligence he understands their responses artistically and humanly recognizes what they express.

* * *

The therapist will find that group activities are golden opportunities for therapy. When he is first confronted by a group of children, it may seem to be an admixture of pathologies and impairments. But it will not take many sessions of work for him to discover, living within the outward manifestations of damage, the individuality of each child. This is what he is reaching for; this is what he will work with.

In the early sessions both children and therapist need to become free, need to get to know each other. Meanwhile they are having their new musical experiences. As it becomes possible to give the sessions some structure through the repetitions of songs and activities, the relationship between the children and the therapist will become an increasingly friendly sharing of pleasurable, meaningful experience. Then the time will come when the group is ready for a particular form of activity. This may be a number of songs in which the children have instrumental parts to play, it may be a combination of song and story with instruments depicting characters or it may be a dramatic experience with incidental music. The therapist can find guidance for his work by using suitably composed or arranged, well-tested materials. Through the children's responses to them therapeutic goals will become apparent; through his experiences in working with them he will apprehend both musical and practical principles of group activity. The children will inspire him to use these principles resourcefully.

In his work with the group he should never lose sight of the individual child; each child's needs, as well as his abilities should become a vital part of any structured activity in whatever way is possible. Each newly-activated individuality will contribute to the evolution of a special entity with its own unique character—*that particular group of children working together*. When the activity in which the therapist involves them is musically alive, all the children will respond and their responses will enrich each other. In this interplay of responsiveness the group will "reverberate" to experience.

* * *

If he possesses compositional and improvisational abilities the therapist will find the essence of music as therapy to lie in his improvisational creation of music as a language of communication between him and an individual child. The "words" of this language are the components of music at his disposal, its expressive content is carried by his use of them. In the clinical situation he becomes a centre of musical responsiveness himself; the music his fingers draw from the instrument arises from his impressions of the child: facial expression, glance, posture, behaviour, condition—all express that presence his music will reflect and go out to meet. The flexibility of his playing searches out the region of contact for that child, creates the emotional substance of the contact and sets the musical ground for inter-activity. The timing of his playing—its tempo, its rhythms and pauses—attentively follows, leads and follows the child's activity. He enters into the scope and meaning of the child's activity, supporting the experience it carries; his capacity for musical expressiveness in his playing and his singing is at the service of the child's involvement.

Session follows session, the themes and idioms he creates develop and are transformed as the child's activities expand. His improvising is free of any restrictions of conventional musical form for it must constantly meet the changing forms of the child's response. Yet a certain musical structure, unpre-meditated and unforeseeable, evolves through the continuity of the sessions, a structure created by the path and the content of the child's progress. As he leads and follows the child into new regions of self-expression, into new discoveries of freedom, his joy is in the child's joy, his fulfilment in the child's fulfilment. The relationship he has to the child's self-creating self through the creative effort of his music-making, gives his own musical nature—and with it the art of music—a new moral reality in the world.

* * *

In individual therapy and in group activities the therapist must believe in the intrinsic importance of each life with which he is working. He must respect the inward experiences of that life and feel reverence—and enthusiasm—for the freshness of emotional experience that his work can bring to birth in each child. The music therapist who has these feelings for the children and the work he does with them, will find his love for music fired anew. These are the well-springs in which his inspirations arise, the inspirations that become—through the children's activities and his—therapy.

APPENDIX 1

1. This severely brain-damaged boy, for whom an educational programme and most social situations were totally meaningless, wished to "play" the piano with the therapist. He responded strongly to a Spanish idiom and found in his own impulsive piano-playing a direct means of expressing the emotional intensity of his experience. His interest became focused on the therapist who was creating this meaningful, satisfying contact with him.

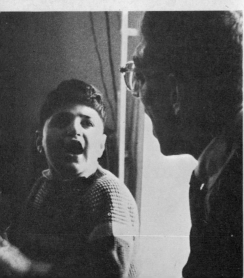

Spontaneously, his vigorous inner energy took expression in free wordless song. The therapist's response answered and supported his outburst. As he sang with and to the therapist, he projected himself intensely into a completely new experience of human relationship.

2.

The "Bell Tree" was created for this sensitive mongoloid boy. He adopted it immediately. In the tonal qualities of the bells and of the piano accompaniment, his capacity for quiet, delicate concentration could unfold. The spatial arrangement of the bells enhanced their differences in pitch.

He plays freely over the whole tree, carefully striking bells one by one.

From time to time he grasps the central branch and, shaking the tree, rings all the bells together.

3.

A moment of awareness and discovery. This emotionally disturbed, brain-damaged boy is overcoming his compulsive beat by finding and beating the melodic rhythm of a song improvised in therapy. He begins to feel the pleasure of expressive freedom. The position of his right foot indicates the quality of his concentration.

4.

A severely retarded mongoloid boy, usually passive and disinterested in human contact, is enthusiastically caught up in his musical activity. His responses are ebulliently creative.

"Wait!"   "Play!"

5.

A seven-year-old emotionally disturbed, aphasoid girl lives intensely in the total experience of self-expression through creation. As she improvises, moment by moment she forms her music, brings her feelings to consciousness and finds words to express herself. At each instant she is aware of the harmonic/melodic forms of the therapist's improvised accompaniment.

In this creative moment all her resources are focused into forming a statement of her inner life.

Totally involved in achieving expression, she pours her feelings into her singing.

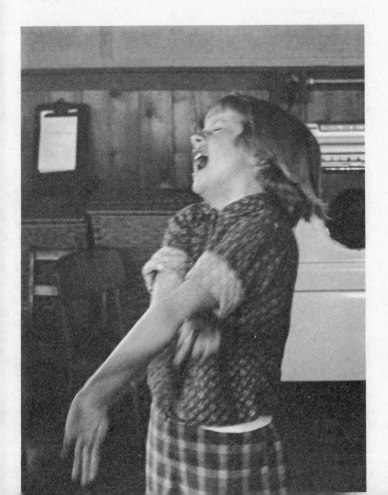

6.

This series of photographs of the seven-year-old autistic girl identified as Rosita on pages 102 to 104, were taken a few days before the breakthrough into song described in her case-study. The pictures were taken at approximately two-minute intervals. The build up of response that led to the singing is well illustrated.

This is how the sessions began at that time. Often a confusion of anticipation and uneasiness produced outward signs of resistance or remoteness.

She is becoming engaged and is being drawn into the activity. Her musical experiences are not yet in the foreground of her mind, they live in the background and have to be brought into focus by the therapist in each session. This is beginning to happen in this picture.

Now living intensely in the rhythmic-emotional experience, stimulated by the improvisation and the therapist's singing, she beats an impulsive *crescendo* on her drum. But it is important to note that the scope of her experience lies within her own psyche. She is caught up in her own internal excitement and pleasure.

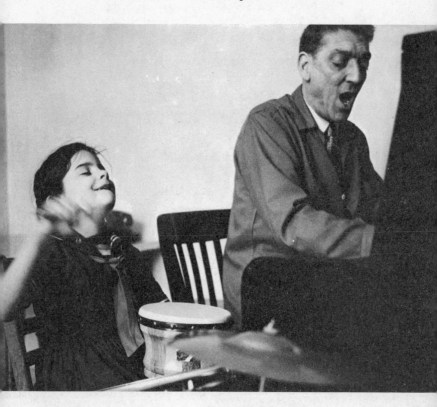

But her beating unites her with the therapist's playing. As he accompanies her impulsive beating, her internal experience becomes supported by his musical enthusiasm. She turns to him and *shares* her experience with him. This unity of her pleasure and his music creates a vital emotional-musical bond between them. They can begin to *work together* and she experiences the animation and freedom that are going to impel her to sing.

Her pleasure and interest become totally outwardly directed. Awakened and concentrated, securely held in the mobile, rich experiences she is having, aware of, trusting, and enjoying the therapist, she leaves the small drum which was her former security and enjoys the tone of the cymbal.

7.

The behaviour of this totally speechless, aphasoid, severely autistic boy was almost entirely compulsive. After five weeks of therapy his consciousness began to be illumined by a dawning recognition of song. Within his fragmented, dislocated psyche emotional responses were born. These were of such original purity that his behaviour was completely changed in the moments of experience. In the photograph he is living in the therapist's voice, rapt in the experience of a thoughtful, tender song.

8.

This blind, aphasoid, withdrawn boy displayed a compulsive beat that approximated 14 beats per minute. This was due to two factors: the inertia he had to overcome to make any physical act, and his super-sensitivity to sound. He used his ears to give him information about objects in terms of their timbre and resonance to an exaggerated degree. He savoured the sounds of music rather than experienced its living expressiveness.

As can be seen from the photograph, early music therapy with this boy was like a game of chess. The deliberation that went into each response is apparent in his total posture. The therapist is also poised, waiting for his response before the next clinical-creative step can be taken.

The aim was to free him from living in the attenuation of isolated notes and to bring him to experiences of tempo and rhythmic form. If this could be achieved he would feel, for the first time in his life, the emotions dependent on *movement* in music. This was achieved by imbuing tonal phrases with rhythmic meaning, by the use of vibrato and rhythmic pulsation in the therapist's singing, and through inciting him into a playful give-and-take. This became therapeutic for his overall emotional development.

9.

Blind, cerebral palsied, and mentally and speech handicapped, this girl lived in restricted isolation. In music therapy she found an organization of expression and experience in which inherent capacities could unfold. This began in song. In using her voice—initially her only means of expressive response—she showed considerable musical perceptiveness, musical intelligence, and a creative tonal sense. She understood the freedom of the improvisational musical situation and used it. Her experiences enlivened her and in co-creativity with the therapist her ego-activity became engaged.

She began to use her capacities with a completely new purposefulness. In moments of attainment and fulfilment she experienced herself with confident certainty. This was further emphasized as she discovered in her arms the means of expressing the rhythmic basis of the songs she had come to love. At times of intensive concentration she discovered and experienced the relationship between melody, words, tempo, and her own expressive capacities—singing, word-formation, drum and cymbal-beating. She effected a synthesis of her capacities through a consciously grasped musical synthesis. As her ego-activity achieved this integration, her mental, emotional, and physical experiences of herself created new developments in her personality. Later she took her co-ordination on to a higher level. This is shown in the photograph where she is beating with right and left hands alternately while singing one of her songs.

10

This three-and-a-half-year-old is having his first music therapy session. He has been diagnosed as being severely retarded and autistic. For about half the session he was inactive but then responded to the therapist's playful but vigorous techniques. The photograph shows the high-spot of the session. There is no trace of autism at this moment and the alertness and energetic intention in the child's face leads one to question the element of retardation. The therapist and the child are playing a musical game, exchanging rapid bursts of piano-playing and drum-beating.

The photograph illustrates the therapeutic opportunities that music therapy offers for disturbed children to bring into action the essentially "normal" part of themselves unrestricted by pathological conditions. These initial moments of release and response can open the way for wide processes of emergent development. This child's consistent ego-development through music therapy compensated for the previous developmental arrest due to organic impairment. He made rapid gains in the use of language and in sustaining personal relationships. In twenty-four months of treatment he outgrew individual music therapy. At the age of six he was taking part in quite complex group activities. He has proved to be educable.

The work being done in the photograph is, in a sense, pre-rhythmic. Work with such young children's incipient responses often demands a highly sensitive, mercurial technique.

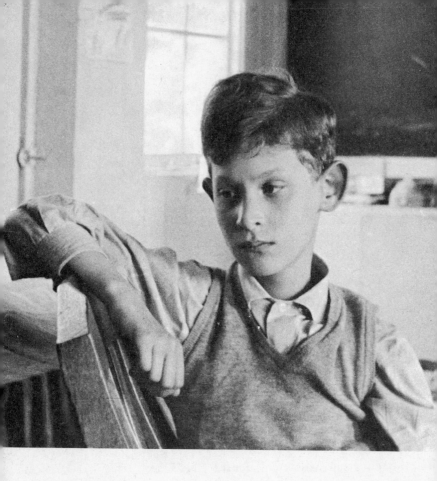

This brain-damaged pre-psychotic boy was too fearful and anxious to use an instrument. He listens meditatively to the poignant music improvised for him.

APPENDIX 11

Pif-Paf-Poltrie

David, as "Pif-Paf-Poltrie", has almost finished his sweeping. The mess was originally quite extensive and covered the floor as far as the circle of children who are sitting around him. It has taken him about ten minutes so far. He has been sweeping diligently all this time. The other children have watched him attentively.

His utter devotion to the sweeping is obvious in the photograph. The quality of perceptive, delicate care is apparent in his arms and hands and in the poised position of his feet. The quality of the mood that prevails in the room is conveyed by the contemplative attitude of the girl near the piano and by the watchfulness with which the therapist is accompanying each sweep that David makes with the besom.

Singing

After a *Pif-Paf* we sing the *Good-bye Song*. It has been a particularly good and lively session and the children spontaneously gather round the piano to sing. The enthusiasm and goodwill with which they sing is very evident: they are putting their hearts into it.

Children want to sing: they have an inherent love of music which they want to express in the activity of singing. If the songs are right they can do this. The words have to be immediately meaningful so that the singers can feel their meaning at the moment they sing them. The melodic-rhythmic setting of the words, and the tempo in which they are sung must be right for the children and for the mood of the song. The harmonies must sustain the mood and support and enliven the melody—so supporting and enlivening the singers. Then the children will feel that the songs are *theirs* and will sing themselves as they sing their songs.

The Three Bears

The children's complete concentration upon what they are doing is apparent in each photograph. The story is enjoyable, the music stimulating, the presentation lively—but the work is highly structured. The children's faces show that they are living in an experience that is bigger than the parts they play. This makes their parts more meaningful and more important. Each instrumental part is musically attractive and dramatically essential to the story; it is set into the form created by the songs, the story-telling, and the accompanying music. It is the children's pleasure but also their *responsibility* to add their individual parts to the whole. They grow to feel this and strive to accomplish it.

Phil plays "two-drums" in *Three Hairy, Furry Bears*, the march that brings the Bears home from the woods.

At definite moments in the same song, Robert holds a long note on the reed-horn.

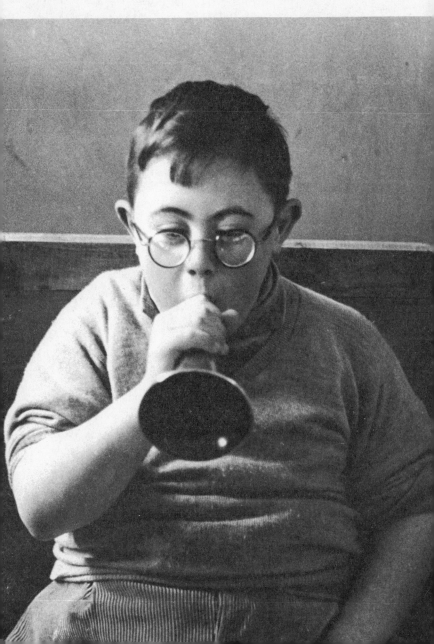

Working on *The Bears' Song* in the classroom. "Father Bear" plays, "Mother Bear" and "Baby Bear" watch the leader for their cues to play. *Photo, Schima Kaufman.*

Goldilocks Had A Shadow. "Goldilocks" is skipping; Louise plays a descending *glissando* on a pentatonically-tuned lyre. Patty waits, poised to play the "Shadow's" skip on a diatonically-tuned toy harp.

The variety of musical sounds of good quality instruments adds an important dimension to the children's experience of the work.

Joshua Fought the Battle of Jericho

The three reed-horns are blown solo and in unison. The drum and the cymbal add dramatic atmosphere. *Photo, Jack De Frenes, Philadelphia.*

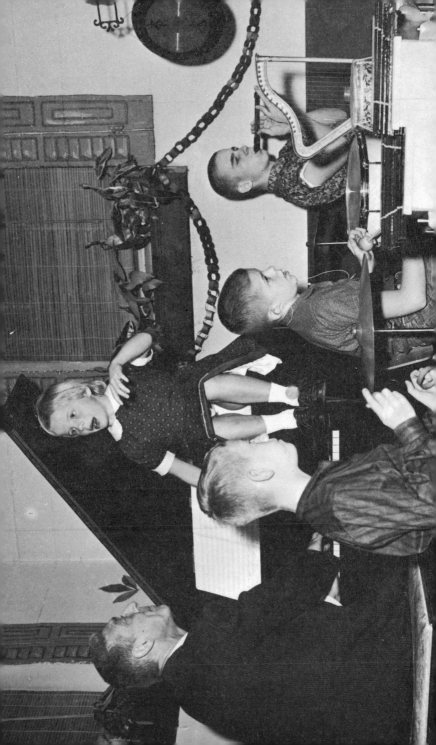

hist-whist

The three boys had "graduated" from individual music therapy: in exploratory sessions each one had shown complete rhythmic freedom. The girl had completed an intensive course of individual therapy and was now ready for group activities.

For these children a special group work, a setting of e. e. cummings' poem *hist-whist*, was composed. In it the three boys played seventeen instruments. A high degree of organization and alertness was required to change quickly from one instrument to another and to play the tricky parts with rhythmic accuracy and a feeling of ensemble. The girl's part was equally advanced, as befitted her exceptional musical gifts. She sang and spoke the words of the poem with rhythmic vitality. At times her part was a solo, at other times she sang or spoke antiphonally or in unison with the pianist.

The piece took three-and-a-half minutes to perform, but eight sessions, each an hour and fifteen minutes in length, were required to perfect it. This is where the therapy lay. Once weekly the "sextet" met and worked hard without pause, learning and practicing the piece, section by section. The children accepted the therapists' single-minded purposefulness in the same spirit; they shared their enthusiasm and gave themselves completely to the hard musical work the piece demanded. Observers of the sessions, who knew the children, were incredulous over their capacity to sustain this kind of complete concentration for over an hour.

This emphasizes one of the most fundamental properties of group music therapy: the opportunities it offers for purposeful, rewarding *work*. It is an everyday experience that handicapped children like music, that music "gets through" to them; it is demonstrable that many are able to partake in musical activities with considerable freedom from pathological impairment. This being so, the therapeutic possibilities of music can be more extensively realized by composing or arranging musical activities that will activate children's capacities as intensively as possible and engage them in the purposeful building-up of well-integrated musical experiences. *Photo, Institute of Logopedics.*

The Story of Artaban

A scene from *The Story of Artaban, the Other Wise Man*. This play, an adaptation of Henry van Dyke's story, *The Other Wise Man*, was written especially for a group of variously handicapped aphasoid youngsters. The simple but dignified speech parts were woven into a fabric of music; music supported the rhythm and dynamics of the speech chorus; frequently, to musical cues, the actors spoke their lines in a kind of recitative. A soprano sang an opening and closing processional song. At one point a dramatic commentary was made in dialogue between the actors and the singer. The piano part was augmented by a drum and orchestral cymbal played by a musical boy with a loss of hearing. Music set the mood throughout the play and supported its entire structure.

The dramatic seriousness of the story appealed to these adolescent children. In the rehearsals they worked hard at overcoming speech impediments. A purposeful, working mood evolved which began to free them from inhibitions and routine adaptive behaviour.

As the play gained momentum its influence spread in the lives of the children. House-mothers taught lines, speech therapists worked on pronunciation and there was even some formal education in the reading of scripts and in the discussions of many scenes in the play. Friends of the Institute volunteered to make the costumes.

The effect of all this upon the youngsters was to widen their horizons of life and supplement their rehabilitation programme with experiences that developed emotional maturity and which, at the same time, strengthened ego function, particularly in those regions where it was most needed and where it had always functioned against handicaps. The children stood up to the inevitable challenge of final rehearsals, taking direction and even criticism objectively, and gave a first performance that astonished and moved the audience of friends, therapists, house-mothers and teachers.

The therapeutic impact of the play lay in both rehearsals and performance, the performance being the summation of a therapeutic process that had its origin and development in the rehearsals. The play became a special world for the youngsters; they realized all manner of developments in working within it. They did this together, each unself-consciously inspiring the other by his own example, each supporting the other with great goodwill and loving loyalty. In this process of mutual growth they became a "cast", a team of performers sharing new experiences that their own efforts made possible. Although they may not have been able to define these experiences, they felt them and were affected by them. After the play was over and the work ended, each one, in his own way, retained its effect in some new measure of self-assurance and happiness. *Photo, Institute of Logopedics.*

A Message for the King

This work for drum ensemble, singers, piano and narrator was composed especially for an older group of Retarded Trainable children. The "King" has played his first section and now watches the conductor. The "Queen" plays her rhythmic pattern to sombre music; in its rests, her "First Son" plays a repeating, answering rhythm. His strong determination to beat despite the handicaps of cerebral palsy is well expressed. The "Second Son", alert for the conductor's cue, waits to beat in unison with the "Queen". *Photo, Kerper's Studio.*

INDEX

References to the illustrated Appendices between pages 144 and 177 are shown in italic, and indicate the caption number in the case of Appendix I, and the title of the group musical activity in the case of Appendix II.

single stringed, in "The Three
 Bears", 24, 127–128,
 Appendix II
vital rhythms of the organism, 52
vitality:
 in improvisations, 103
 threatening to overwhelm, 43

waltz:
 "Beautiful Wendy Is here with
  Me", 79, 82, 83
 carnival, 103
 heavily accented, 80

-song, "Lisa Can Say Hello", 102
Wendy, 75–86
What Shall We Do with the Dog?,
 119
whistles, *see also* flutes, simple
 bamboo, 82
whistling, by child, 81
Wolmut, Felice, 115

xylophone:
 in "hist-whist", *Appendix II*
 in individual therapy, 106,
  108–110